The Analogue Revolution

The Analogue Revolution

Revolution

Communication
Technology 1901 – 1914

Simon Webb

PEN & SWORD
HISTORY

AN IMPRINT OF PEN & SWORD BOOKS LTD.
YORKSHIRE – PHILADELPHIA

First published in Great Britain in 2018 by
Pen & Sword History
An imprint of
Pen & Sword Books Ltd
Yorkshire - Philadelphia

Copyright © Simon Webb, 2018

ISBN 978 1 52671 537 1

The right of Simon Webb to be identified as Author of this work has been asserted by him in
accordance with the Copyright, Designs and Patents Act 1988.

A CIP catalogue record for this book is
available from the British Library.

Printed and bound in England
By TJ International Ltd.

Pen & Sword Books Ltd incorporates the Imprints of Pen & Sword Books Archaeology, Atlas,
Aviation, Battleground, Discovery, Family History, History, Maritime, Military, Naval, Politics,
Railways, Select, Transport, True Crime, Fiction, Frontline Books, Leo Cooper, Praetorian Press,
Seaforth Publishing, Wharncliffe and White Owl.

For a complete list of Pen & Sword titles please contact
PEN & SWORD BOOKS LIMITED
47 Church Street, Barnsley, South Yorkshire, S70 2AS, England
E-mail: enquiries@pen-and-sword.co.uk
Website: www.pen-and-sword.co.uk
or
PEN AND SWORD BOOKS
1950 Lawrence Rd, Havertown, PA 19083, USA
E-mail: Uspen-and-sword@casematepublishers.com
Website: www.penandswordbooks.com

Contents

List of Plates

Introduction

In the last thirty years or so there have been great changes in the way that information is stored and retrieved, and also in the methods by which people communicate with each other. These changes, which began in the industrialized nations of the Western World, have manifested themselves in the ubiquitous appearance of mobile telephones in public places and the universal presence of small, powerful computers in shops, offices, schools and homes. This upheaval in information technology is sometimes called the Digital Revolution or the beginning of the Information Age.

A little over a century ago, a similar transformation took place in the way that information of all kinds was handled and sent from one place to another. Just as during the modern Digital Revolution, the way that images, text, speech and music were recorded and then forwarded to other people underwent a sea change, as did the speed with which communications took place. It was plain to those caught up in this earlier technological revolution that the world had somehow shrunk and that things would never be the same again. Somebody in London could now speak to another person, hundreds of miles away, without even leaving his or her home. Photographs could also be sent from one country to another at the speed of light. The formalities of Victorian letter-writing were dispensed with and a new mode of exchanging text messages evolved; one which entailed arranging to meet later that day by simply a few abbreviated phrases, much as we now use emails, texts and instant messaging services. These simple text messages frequently featured amusing or eye-catching images, just as memes are now spread via social media. Moving images of events around the world could now be viewed by ordinary people within days, or even hours, of their taking place. Most excitingly of all, the various rapid advances in information technology were being combined in strange and wholly unexpected ways. Each day seemed to bring forth new instances of this trend. In our own time, we have seen something similar; a convergence in digital information processing, leading to startling and unlooked-for developments.

At the beginning of the twenty-first century, mobile telephones were used for calling people, photographs were taken with cameras and MP3 players were used to listen to music, while those wishing to send an email were usually obliged to wait until they got home and could use a computer. Today, almost everybody carries around a miniature computer which can record films, play music and provide instant access to that vast collection of computers known as the Internet. One can also, of course, make telephone calls with it. Precisely the same thing happened in Britain during the first fifteen years of the twentieth century, as one innovation was harnessed to another, with astonishing results.

Some of the world's first radio broadcasts of speech and music were made in 1906 and 1907, with music provided by gramophone records. A novel combination of two new media led to a completely new experience for people in their homes. A few years later, there was an even more intriguing example of this sort of thing when, on 21 April 1913, King George V crossed the English Channel on the Royal Yacht on his way to Paris. As he disembarked at Calais, an aeroplane flew overhead, filming the scene for a newsreel company. The plane travelled straight to Hendon aerodrome on the outskirts of London, from where the canister containing the film was rushed to a laboratory to be developed. At 5.20 pm that same day, audiences at the London Coliseum were able to view events which had taken place on the other side of the Channel a matter of hours earlier.

We sometimes forget how much of our Digital Revolution is founded upon ideas and technical devices which were first developed during the Edwardian Era. The Internet, for example, relies upon a vast and intricate network of fibre-optic cables, many of them laid beneath the sea, to carry information to and from our computers and mobiles. These cables operate by means of pulses of light which carry telephone calls, texts, emails, music, films and a thousand-and-one other things from one end of the Earth to the other. It all sounds very advanced and ultra-modern and yet the basic principles behind the system were being exploited well over a century ago.

As early as June 1880 Alexander Graham Bell, inventor of the telephone, demonstrated the wireless transmission of speech by means of a modulated beam of light. He believed this invention to be even more important than the telephone which he had patented a few years earlier. An early version of Bell's Photophone, which shows speech being transmitted along a beam of light, may be seen in Illustration 1. Others working in this field at the time called this the 'radiophone'. Today, we use the light from lasers to send the telephone calls, television programmes and other things along the fibre-optic cables, but of course there were no lasers in those days. In the opening years of the twentieth century, the most powerful light sources were carbon arc lamps and using these, it was found possible to send telephone messages for five miles or more.

Another example of the way in which the modern world has been shaped by the technological developments of the Edwardian period may be seen in the hard drives which store information on our computers. These are magnetized discs, upon which information is recorded by passing electromagnetic impulses from a stylus which is placed above the spinning disc of the hard drive. This too is no more than a recent development of a system first devised in 1899. It was in that year that the world's first magnetic recording machine was patented, using steel wire to record speech. Later versions of this device used steel discs instead of wire and these were used in a very primitive, but effective, telephone answering machine. By 1904, telephones were being answered automatically at England's Royal Dockyards and the spoken messages stored on discs by means of this recording system. A drawing from the patent for this early system may be seen in Illustration 2.

These early devices were all analogue, rather than digital. Digital recordings of music were, however, also being made at that time. Edvard Grieg, the Norwegian composer and pianist, died in 1907, but there exist recordings of him playing his own compositions. The analogue recordings of that time, on wax cylinders and shellac discs, are almost unbearably crackly and distorted. Not so the digital music, which is as crisp and clear as when Grieg sat down at the piano to record it in 1905.

The roots of our modern Information Revolution are to be found in the Edwardian Era. Not only was much of our technology first seen at that time, but the Edwardians experienced many of the difficulties which we have seen in recent years, when society comes to terms with changing circumstances and the old ways of doing things seem to become obsolete almost overnight. From worries about children giving up reading in favour of new media which monopolize their leisure time, to the anxiety that the English language was deteriorating due to its increasingly slovenly use in informal modes of communication, the Edwardians tackled these same problems over a century ago.

Before examining in detail what might be termed the Edwardian Analogue Revolution, it might be wise to remind readers just what is meant by analogue information systems, as opposed to the digital forms which have now almost wholly replaced them.

An analogue is nothing more than a representation or copy of something. Using a manual typewriter, for instance, resulted in the metal print-head striking an inky tape and leaving a copy of itself on the paper. Using an old-fashioned photocopier to make a copy of a typed document would cause an analogue or copy of the printing to be created on an electrically-charged metal cylinder and then transferred to another sheet of paper. The same system of making representations or copies was used in traditional radio broadcasting or speaking on the telephone. When one speaks, a longitudinal wave is formed in the air, with the molecules of gas compressed together most where the sound is loudest and these compressions separated by more tenuous spaces which indicate a reduced volume or even silence. When a wave of this kind strikes an analogue microphone, say in the mouthpiece of a telephone, the compressed parts of the air cause a stronger electric current to flow along the wire from the microphone. These surges precisely mimic the original sound waves, forming an analogue of the original compression wave in the varying current which travels along the wire to recreate the sound in the earpiece at the other end of the line.

Digital communication and storage systems, on the other hand, convert the original data not into copies, but rather a stream of digits; the ones and zeros of binary mathematics. Sound waves are sampled thousands of times a second and the digital measurements are sent as a series of pulses which are reconstructed at the other end. Analogue data transmitted in the form of waves is easily distorted, resulting in crackly and imprecise reception. Copied text may also become blurred, photographs fade and gramophone records become scratched. None of this happens with digital information, which is why it has replaced analogue recording and communication throughout the world.

If we are going to examine the Edwardian information revolution, then it might be profitable for us to pause and consider just what we mean by the expression 'information revolution'. What *is* an information revolution and why should such a thing have any great effect upon those living in an age when one is under way? In the first chapter, we shall be looking at Edwardian society and seeing some of the ways that the revolution in analogue devices affected the lives of the Edwardians. The next chapter will then examine the nature of information revolutions in general and see why the one which took place in the first fourteen years of the twentieth century was of particular significance.

Chapter 1

The Edwardian World

L.P. Hartley famously observed that, 'The past is a foreign country; they do things differently there'. This may make for a neat sound bite, but it is not really true. People in any age have much the same urges and desires; they hanker after what are essentially the same things. They all want security, a home of their own, sufficient resources that they will not go hungry, the opportunity to start a family of their own and perhaps to be given the chance to avail themselves of some of the luxuries of the day. Of course, the particular objects of their desires, beyond these bare essentials, will change radically from century to century. For an Anglo–Saxon peasant, glass in his windows and a hot bath once a week would have been unimaginable luxury, whereas today we might dream of the latest iPhone or a fairy-tale wedding in a Scottish castle. What we consider as luxuries may vary dramatically over the decades and centuries, but the basic wish for a home of our own, food on the table and a secure life have remained unchanged for thousands of years.

From this perspective, we can begin with the assumption that the men and women in Edwardian Britain were not so very different from us. That period is close enough in time to make their world recognizable to us, as many of what we have come now to regard as the basic necessities of life, things such as electricity, telephones and cinema films, were already in existence. In fact, the Edwardian world has a great deal in common with our own. Their reactions to things such as exciting new developments in technology are almost certainly going to be easy for us to understand. It was a time when the world in general, and Britain in particular, was going through great upheavals and social changes, many of which would be all too familiar to us today. Not only this, but the Edwardians were in the midst of an information revolution, with every day bringing forth improvements and new developments in the ways that people communicated with each other or stored data. It was very similar to the so-called digital revolution which is still going on around us, but in the case of the Edwardians, this revolution was not digital, but analogue.

In later chapters, we shall be examining in detail the effect that the Analogue Revolution had upon British society, but to begin with it might be helpful if we look at the world of the Edwardians and see how they lived and what sort of problems they were facing. Doing this will show enormous and uncanny similarities to our own time, with many of what we believe to be modern anxieties and worries already present over a century ago.

The first thing to grasp about Edwardian Britain is that it was a time of great change, with old certainties thrown into the melting pot and ordinary men and women clamouring for a new order, a fresh way of dealing with the problems which had beset the country for many years. The new information and communications technology, which was appearing everywhere at the time, helped to accelerate this process of demand for a new society.

Everywhere at that time was a feeling that life was proceeding at an ever-increasing pace and that the old order was changing with astonishing rapidity. There was a frenzied and hectic air about those years leading up to the First World War and it was this sense of urgency and speed which comes across most clearly when reading descriptions of that period in British history. Key to this haste was the new ways in which people could now communicate with each other. Postcards were being sent by the billion in the first years of the century and T. Corkett, of the largest postcard company in Britain, Raphael Tucker and Sons Ltd, had this to say, 'The postcard is part and parcel of the busy, rushing, time-saving age in which we live.' Novelist James Hilton summed the case up neatly when he wrote of, 'that frenzied Edwardian decade, like an electric lamp which goes brighter and whiter just before it burns itself out'. In short, the defining features of this period were the speed of everyday life and the great changes which were taking place wherever one looked.

This is not at all the image that we many of us have of this period in British history. The very word 'Edwardian' conjures up thoughts of stability and suggests subliminally the idea that we are talking about the high-water mark of the British Empire; a kind of tranquil, golden era, which was soon to be shattered by the terrible events of the First World War. When we describe something as 'Victorian', there is often a faintly pejorative air about our use of the word. We mean unenlightened, stiff, formal and prudish; Victorian workhouses, Victorian attitudes to sex, Victorian hypocrisy. There are no such negative connotations attached to 'Edwardian'. Our mind drifts unbidden to thoughts of grand garden parties, Henley Regatta, Elgar's symphonies, *Land of Hope and Glory*, high society and richly-dressed ladies carrying parasols. Illustration 3 shows two Edwardian ladies at 'Glorious Goodwood'. This is the sort of image which many of us associate with Edwardian Britain.

Many of our views and opinions on the nature of Edwardian society come of course not from history books, but rather television programmes such as *Downton Abbey* and *Upstairs, Downstairs*. Stability and order are the chief features of the Edwardian world when viewed from the perspective of such programmes. In films too, Edwardian Britain is a well-to-do place, with even the poor knowing their place and being cheerful about their lives. One thinks of that classic film *Mary Poppins*, with the delightful life of the Banks family. There is a poor man in this film, Bert the chimney sweep, but he is even happier than Mr Banks and his family. He may not have much money, but Bert is forever larking about and having wonderful adventures. We have subliminally absorbed this vision of Edwardian life and unless we take the trouble to seek out the historical reality, that is how we are liable to see this chapter of British history. The truth was very different.

Mary Poppins, which has as a backdrop a delightful, peaceful and picturesque London, was set in 1910. We know this from the words of one of the film's songs. The real London of that year was in the throes of the greatest political and social upheaval seen in Britain for centuries. The confrontations and strikes known as the 'Great Unrest' were reaching their climax and within twelve months the capital would become an armed camp. Over 12,000 troops would be quartered in the parks of central London and in the north of England, and the army would be shooting down men like Bert the chimney sweep as what amounted to martial law was imposed upon the provinces. In Ireland, not at that time an independent country but an integral part of Great Britain, a civil war was brewing. Why then, with so many disturbing things going on, do we persist in viewing Edwardian Britain as a golden era?

There is something dramatically satisfying about comparing the supposedly prosperous and peaceful world of Edwardian Britain in the run-up to 1914, with the massacre of the country's youth at Passchendaele and the Somme. It provides such a stark contrast and serves to underline and accentuate just how horrible the First World War was. In fact, British society in the years preceding the outbreak of war was anything but prosperous and peaceful; many at the time thought that the nation was on the brink of revolution and civil war and the social conditions of millions of people living in Britain at that time were atrocious.

During the nineteenth century, Britain had been the richest country in the world, but of course the wealth was by no means evenly or equitably distributed. Fortunately for those who were well-off, there was still a lingering belief, supported by the Church, that people should be content with their station in life and not seek to rise higher in the social scheme of things than their birth and family circumstances warranted. We hear an echo of the supposedly Divine backing for the existing order in the Victorian hymn *All Things Bright and Beautiful*. One verse sums the matter up in a nutshell, by declaring;

> The rich man in his castle,
> The poor man at his gate,
> God made them high and lowly,
> And ordered their estate.

By the time of Queen Victoria's death in 1901, this old notion of patient resignation to one's situation in life was becoming a little threadbare and with the dawn of a new century, many of the poorer people in Britain were agitating for change. The old certainties were breaking down and when the Liberals swept to power in the landslide victory of 1906, Henry Campbell-Bannerman, the newly-elected Prime Minister, had already promised that things were going to change. He said his aim was to make the country, 'less of a pleasure-ground for the rich and more of a treasure-house for the nation'.

The inequalities at that time really were appalling. During the Boer War, fought in South Africa between 1899 and 1902, there was a surge of patriotic fervour in Britain and a desire to rally to the flag. Of the men who tried to join the army at that time, no fewer than 40 per cent were found to be physically unsuitable; chiefly through being malnourished and undersized. A large proportion of the population were living practically on the edge of starvation. At the turn of the century, Seebohm Rowntree, the Quaker industrialist and social researcher, published the results of his investigations into the conditions of working-class people in the city of York. Called *Poverty; A Study of Town Life*, the report analysed the lives of two-thirds of the population of York. It was found that roughly a third of the people living in York did not have enough food, fuel and clothing to keep them in good health. Even if they carefully spent every single penny, there was still not enough coming in to allow them to live a healthy life. The picture was the same throughout the whole of the country. It was this dreadful situation that the Liberals hoped to tackle.

The popular newspapers, which were now being read by an increasing number of working-class people, made information about things such as Rowntree's study of poverty freely available to everybody. Those struggling to survive knew that they were not isolated cases and that almost the entire working class in Britain was in a desperate position. It also became widely known among such readers that the rich lived lives which were almost inconceivably different from theirs. Reading about, seeing photographs in the newspapers and films at the music hall showing how extravagantly the upper stratum of society was living, could not fail to provoke envy and anger in those struggling to survive perpetually on the edge of starvation.

J.B. Priestley, the well-known author and playwright, gives a vivid description of breakfast at in an upper-class home when guests were staying for a weekend shooting party. This, it must be borne in mind, was at a time when many families were surviving on little more than bread and dripping, that is to say bread smeared with a little animal fat, and a cup or two of tea each day:

> There were pots of coffee and of China and Indian tea, and various cold drinks. One large sideboard would offer a row of silver dishes, kept hot by spirit lamps, and here there would be poached or scrambled eggs, bacon, ham, sausages, devilled kidneys, haddock and other fish. On an even larger sideboard there would be a choice of cold meats – pressed beef, ham, tongue, galantines – and cold roast pheasant, grouse, partridge, ptarmigan. A side table would be heaped with fruit – melons, peaches, nectarines, raspberries. And if anybody was hungry, there were always scone and toast and marmalade and honey and specially imported jams.

The effect of reading about such profligacy by somebody barely able to afford sufficient food to stave off the pangs of hunger is impossible to imagine.

Despite his good intentions Campbell-Bannerman and his successor Henry Herbert Asquith found it easier said than done to transform society. In real terms, wages were falling, but wealthy and aristocratic individuals hardly seemed to notice this. They certainly weren't affected by the depression. Ascot, Henley Regatta and garden parties at Buckingham Palace continued much as they had during Victoria's reign. The difference now was that ordinary working-class people were able to see this conspicuous consumption for themselves.

During the period that Victoria was on the throne, there was every bit as much inequality as was to be found after her son's coronation in 1901. There was one vital difference though. Poor people in the 1850s were largely illiterate and would in any case have been unlikely to have enough money to spare for buying a newspaper. Photography was a novelty and no method yet existed for mass-producing copies of photographs and printing them in newspapers. We shall examine this point at length in a subsequent chapter. Needless to say, there were no cinemas. The result was that men and women working in factories in the north of England or farms in the West Country would have no idea at all what a day out at Ascot actually looked like. Nor would they know whether their own lives were typical of the labouring classes or whether they were just unfortunate enough to be worse off than average.

By the time of the 1906 general election though, tabloid newspapers costing only a halfpenny were circulating widely and they had photographs on their front page, pictures which showed clearly how the 'other half' lived. It was possible now for an errand boy to see just how rich people dressed at Henley and to read also what sort of things they got up to. Celebrity gossip was then, as it is now, a topic of enduring interest to those whose lives are not so showy or exciting. Not only could the people who were feeling the squeeze of falling wages see photographs of tycoons driving motor cars or aristocrats at play, they could even watch moving pictures of them.

When films began to be shown in Britain, towards the end of the nineteenth century, they were typically presented at the end of music-hall shows and consisted in the main of short news items, rather than fictional narratives. These would come later. Those producing these early newsreels thought that viewers would probably prefer to see something a little different from their day-to-day lives and so took their cameras out and about. It was only natural that, in general, ostentatious events such as society weddings and a day out at Ascot would be more likely to be recorded than the interior of a sweatshop or slum tenement. In this way, working men and women were exposed to scenes of luxury and affluence such as they could scarcely imagine. Some of these scenes of upper-class life were even in colour, which must have made them even more impressive. The funeral of Edward VII on 20 May 1910 was filmed by the Natural Colour Kinematograph Co and a spectacular occasion it was too, with no fewer than nine kings being present.

Being able to see what sort of lives were being led by their social superiors helped to create a sense of dissatisfaction among the urban proletariat in particular. It was patently unfair that that while they and their families were going hungry and older relatives were ending up in the workhouse, others in the country were living in such outrageous and unabashed luxury. The emerging phenomenon of the mass media of newspapers and cinema thus served to stoke social unrest. This and other grievances were brought about as a direct consequence of innovations in printing and photography. To see how this process worked, we cast our minds back to the reign of Elizabeth I in the sixteenth century.

In November 1588 a traveller from London arrived at a tavern in an out-of-the-way village in Somerset and discovered to his amazement that those drinking there had no idea what had happened after the Spanish Armada had clashed with the English fleet over three months earlier. The villagers had heard that an invasion fleet had been sighted off the Devon coast in July, but had not the faintest idea what had happened after that. For all they knew to the contrary, King Philip of Spain might now be occupying the throne of England, rather than Queen Elizabeth. With no newspapers and most people spending their whole lives within a few miles of their village or town, news travelled at a snail's pace.

Over the next 300 years, the speed at which news spread across the country increased a little, although most people still relied upon rumour and hearsay to know what was going on in their own country. Victorian newspapers such as the *Times* were not only expensive, but were also very heavy going and anybody with indifferent literacy skills would have found it all but impossible to plough through the verbatim accounts of Parliamentary debates and extract the salient points. Jumping now to the beginning of 1911, and it is at once possible to see how things had changed by then, by looking at another aspect of life in Britain at that time.

Immigration and terrorism were in 1911, just as they are today, matters of great concern to the man and woman in the street. Then, as now, they were linked in the public mind, most terrorists in Britain at that time having been born abroad. How did this become generally known? The answer is of course that the new mass media, to which a great number of working people were now exposed, told them so. After all, nearly all the immigrants in Britain during the opening years of the twentieth century concentrated themselves in specific parts of the big cities such as London and Manchester. People living in the West Country or on the south coast would be unlikely ever to meet one of these foreigners. They knew all about them though from articles in the new popular newspapers which began appearing at about that time. These newspapers put news into simple and straightforward terms and illustrated it with photographs. The *Daily Mirror* and *Daily Sketch,* which began respectively in 1903 and 1909, gave people a highly simplified and sometimes tendentious version of what was going on in the world.

The illustrated newspapers combined with an entirely new mass medium, that of the cinema film, to ensure that every person, even the illiterate, could now see what was going on at the other end of the country in a matter of hours. In doing so, these new media found that they were not only informing readers and viewers; they were at the same time shaping their opinions.

In December 1910 a gang of asylum seekers were breaking into a jeweller's shop in the city of London one night, when they were disturbed by a group of police officers. The burglars were trying to raise funds for a terrorist group and were well-armed. They shot their way out of trouble, killing three police officers in the process. Even without encouragement, most people would have taken a dim view of such antics, but the *Daily Mirror* did not help matters by shrieking, 'Who are these fiends in human form?' The paper offered a reward of £500 for the capture of the murderers. When the killers were finally tracked down to a house in Sidney Street in the East End of London, they fired on the police who came to arrest them. A stand-off developed, which became known as the Siege of Sidney Street or the Battle of Stepney. Troops were called in by Home Secretary Winston Churchill, who also summoned artillery to the scene with a view to having the house where the assassins were hiding shelled. As it was, they were killed in the gun battle with the soldiers, following which the house caught fire.

The affair in Sidney Street was captured by a film crew for the Pathé news company and the footage shown at music halls across the country. What would once have passed without notice by ordinary working men and women, other than those living in the surrounding streets, was now a matter of concern to people everywhere in Britain. Of course, a century earlier The *Times* would have reported such an outrage, but newspapers were too expensive for most people to afford. Because cinema films and newsreels such as this were seen, by and large, only by working-class people, this new medium began to shape how the ordinary men and women, the vast majority of people in the country, saw things. The new, cheap and illustrated newspapers told them that the men responsible for the murders of the police officers and the necessity of calling out the military in London were foreigners and now they could see for themselves what these foreigners had been up to. They learned how many people were coming into the country each year and what the result of that influx might mean for them, perhaps lower wages and more overcrowded living conditions. They even learned what the Home Secretary looked like!

When Winston Churchill arrived at Sidney Street to direct operations, he was immediately recognized by the crowds gathered there, who greeted him with boos and cries of, 'Who let them in?', a reference to the supposed failure of the Home Office to control immigration from Eastern Europe. It is very unlikely that a century earlier, a London crowd would have recognized Viscount Sidmouth had he appeared in the street. It is entirely possible that even his name would be unfamiliar to most people and that hardly anybody would even know that he was the Home Secretary. It was the cheap newspapers, combined with the newly devised method of halftone photographs, which meant that pictures of politicians could now be printed in newspapers, which led to Churchill's being so readily identified. For instance, the *Daily Illustrated Mirror* had covered most of their front page with a wonderfully clear engraving of Winston Churchill as early as 1904. Since then, photographs of him had appeared regularly in the new mass-circulation newspapers. No wonder then that he was immediately recognized when he turned up at Sidney Street.

The year that began with the Siege of Sidney Street was the climax of what became known as the 'Great Unrest'. Across the whole of Britain, but particularly in industrial and mining areas, people were expressing their dissatisfaction with the social and political system in the country. Here too, the new mass media were influential not just in recording but also shaping the course of events. The mood of discontent showed itself in various practical ways, chief among which were striking and rioting. In Victorian Britain, troops could be despatched to deal with unrest without anybody much noticing or objecting, but this was no longer the case. By 1911, the sight of soldiers on the streets would be sure to attract the attention of a film crew and then a few days later music hall audiences across the length and breadth of the land would be seeing what was going on, on the streets of Liverpool or London. This could inflame those living in other parts of the country and lead to what we now call 'copycat riots'.

In the summer of 1911 there were dock strikes in both London and Liverpool. During Queen Victoria's reign, such industrial action would have been unknown to the average working-class person outside those cities. Obviously, the *Times* and perhaps the *Daily Telegraph* would have reported it, but such news would only have been read by comfortably-off professionals or members of the middle classes. Even then, photographs of the events would not have been seen by many people. How very different was the situation in 1911. Pathé newsreel camera crews captured the strikes and the reaction of the authorities as it all unfolded. These films were shown in music halls and cinemas a few days later, keeping everybody fully informed about what was going on.

There is of course sometimes a fine line between reporting news and actually creating it. In Edwardian Britain, with the mass media still something of a novelty, this line was frequently crossed. When thinking up a title for a short piece of film about strikes and sporadic outbreaks of rioting, it is possible to think of many neutral descriptions which might fit the case. The one chosen when the newsreel was shown to working-class audiences across the country could hardly have been more provocative. The caption at the beginning declared 'CIVIL WAR. London and Liverpool under Mob Law'.

The scenes in the film did not seem to indicate anything even remotely approaching a civil war. Police officers were shown escorting horse-drawn carts driven by strike-breakers, which were removing provisions from a London railway station, and in Liverpool columns of mounted troops were shown, trotting sedately through the streets. It all looked very peaceable. It was almost as though the cameraman had been disappointed to find things so quiet and decided to spice up his film a little with a lurid headline.

Later that summer, there was indeed violence, with troops opening fire on strikers, but it was thought that the newsreels of the early part of the strike had acted to inflame the situation, by creating a sense of emergency where none existed. Were these films recording news or helping to shape it?

After the worst of the rioting that summer had subsided, schoolboys began their own disturbances in many parts of Britain. These disturbances were at the time attributed to some observers as being a direct consequence of the news coverage of earlier violence. In August 1911, there were several deaths during the rioting, with troops firing on crowds in Liverpool and also Llanelli in Wales. These deaths and detailed accounts of the rioting which preceded them, were dutifully recorded in the new, popular newspapers such as the *Daily Mirror*, *Daily Sketch* and so on. Because they had such high circulations among working men and women, when schoolboys throughout the country organized what became known as the 'School Strikes', it was widely suspected that they had been prompted to do so by having seen the images from the rioting that adults had been engaging in a few weeks earlier. In other words, they were no more than what we now call 'copycat riots'.

On 5 September, a group of boys marched out of their school in the Welsh town of Llanelli, to protest about the caning of a pupil by an assistant teacher. In a matter of days, similar actions had taken place in sixty towns throughout Britain. It was improbable in the extreme that these widespread protests had erupted spontaneously. It was also very unlikely that some mastermind among the schoolboys had managed to coordinate so many actions by telephone! The only logical conclusion was that it was seeing photographs and reading about the events in Llanelli which had put the idea into the minds of other children. It is hard to see how schoolchildren in Liverpool, Glasgow, Sheffield and Birmingham would all have got it into their heads to play truant *en masse,* unless they picked up the idea from the newspapers reporting similar events elsewhere.

The 'School Strikes' were just one more manifestation of the discontent felt by many people, young and old, in Edwardian Britain. There can be little doubt that the new mass media of cinema and newspapers played their part in spreading radical and exciting new ideas. Those who had previously followed the Victorian ideology of being satisfied with their station in life were no longer ready to follow this way of thinking. Hungry people were seeing that some of those living in their country had more to eat for breakfast than many families could expect to enjoy for the entire week. When troops were mobilized for strike-breaking or counter-terrorism operations, moving pictures of them would be seen by many people within days. It would perhaps be an exaggeration to say that the newspapers and cinema *caused* the unrest which swept the nation in the years leading up to the First World War, but there can be no denying that they played a significant role in what happened.

The supposed role of cheap newspapers in destabilizing society had been feared for hundreds of years before Edward VII came to the throne. We shall be examining in some detail in this book the so-called 'taxes on knowledge', by which successive governments in London had done their best to prevent ordinary people from having free access to ideas or even news. Briefly, newspapers were thought by the authorities in England in the eighteenth and nineteenth centuries to be fomenting discontent and encouraging disorder, by making ordinary people dissatisfied with their lot. It wasn't so bad when only wealthy and well-educated people could read about the state of affairs in this country and abroad, but poor people would start growing restless and unhappy if they thought about the state of the world too much.

Between 1712, when the Stamp Act was passed, and 1855, when all such taxes ended, a series of laws was passed which imposed taxes on paper, printed matter and advertisements. The effect was to make newspapers too expensive for the average person, thus preventing most people in Britain from learning about what was going on in both their own country and abroad. Even knowing what was being said in Parliament was thought to be a threat to the established order. In 1738, a law was passed which made it illegal to publish reports of debates in Parliament and anybody seen making notes in the public gallery was thrown out. All this was explicitly aimed at preventing the spread of domestic news. It was believed by the government of the day to be dangerous for ordinary citizens to read what MPs were saying in the House of Commons.

With the explosive expansion of newspaper-reading during the Edwardian period, it was seen that perhaps those who had had reservations about the effects of widespread knowledge of what was going on had a point! Whatever one's views on the ethics of deliberately withholding knowledge about current affairs from the great mass of the population might be, there can be no doubt that once the floodgates were opened and newspapers became cheap enough for all to afford, the effects upon society were dramatic and wide-ranging. In a very real sense, newspapers and cinema shaped Britain in the years running up to the First World War. Examining one example of this in detail will show what was going on at that time.

When the Houndsditch murders and the siege of Sidney Street took place over the final weeks of 1910 and the first few days of 1911, unease about the number of foreigners entering Britain had been growing for years. Many refugees, people we would today call asylum-seekers, had been seeking sanctuary in this country following troubles in Russia and Eastern Europe. Most of these newcomers were Jews, who tended to concentrate in certain parts of big cities like London and Manchester. In London, Whitechapel virtually became a ghetto, where few English families lived. They had a strange religion, spoke a different language and ate unfamiliar food. And there seemed to be an awful lot of them! Not only that, the new community seemed to be sheltering terrorists and criminals. According to the newspapers, the crime rate was now rising, an increase due to the presence of so many foreigners, or so it was alleged.

The Pathé newsreels of the Siege of Sidney Street, showing troops fighting a gun battle on the streets of the capital, exchanging shots with foreign Jews, did not go down well with many people. They began to ask why all these people should be coming to their country. The newsreels shown at the many new cinemas could not help but create unease about immigration. Newspapers did not exactly help the situation. Often, they encouraged people to see foreigners and Jews as being the enemy within; terrorists, criminals and men who were taking jobs away from Englishmen in their own country. These sentiments were being fostered by both local and national newspapers.

Following the Siege of Sidney Street and the unrelated murder of a Jew, whose body was found on Clapham Common in south London, two local newspapers in London made their own feelings plain. The *East London Observer* said of the Whitechapel district in January 1911 that:

It is doubtful if there is more than a score of English families living within a radius of 500 yards of Sidney Street. Certainly, there is not a single English tradesman there; the public houses are tenanted by Jews and foreigners, and foreign drinks are almost solely consumed.

The newspaper covering that part of London containing Clapham Common, where the body of Leon Beron, a Russian-born Jew who had been murdered by another foreign-born Jew, had been discovered on New Year's Day 1911, carried a stern editorial. The *South-Western Star* said:

> Why should people who have murders to do invade a select neighbourhood like Clapham? Above all, why should alien Jews come here? We sincerely hope that neither Clapham nor Battersea is about to be overrun with undesirables as other parts of London have been.

The conflation of Jews and foreigners was ominous in these newspaper articles. Jews had been living happily in Britain for centuries; one, Benjamin Disraeli, had even become Prime Minister. Now, the idea began to grow that Jews were essentially alien outsiders. Newspaper articles such as those above played on this theme. Even straightforward reports of the debates in Parliament had the effect of working up fears about foreigners in general and Jews in particular.

Pogroms in Russia and Poland had been causing many people, an awful lot of them Jews, to seek refuge in Britain. The levels of net immigration at that time were astonishing, dwarfing anything we have seen in recent years. On 8 February 1911, Home Secretary Winston Churchill was asked some hard questions about this in the House of Commons. An MP called Croft asked the Home Secretary just how many foreigners were entering the United Kingdom. The answer was that in 1910, 600,000 had come to the country; over half a million in one year alone. This certainly puts modern British fears about immigration in perspective! No question in 1911 of net migration to Britain being reduced to the tens of thousands, a key mantra for successive Conservative governments in recent years. Another MP asked Churchill if it was true that the crime rate had fallen towards the end of the nineteenth century and was now rising, due to the many foreigners convicted of various offences. Another question dealt with people-trafficking. The Home Secretary admitted that this had been a problem, with large groups of people being smuggled into the country, but he claimed that the problem was now under control. Yet another question dealt with the idea that foreigners were entering the country to obtain medical treatment, what we would today call 'health tourism'.

There is, for the modern reader, something strikingly familiar about all this. Porous borders, which allow uncontrolled immigration into Britain which the government seem wholly unable to get a grip on; people-smugglers; health tourism; the development of parallel communities, whose members have little contact with mainstream society and which apparently shelter terrorists; Eastern European workers coming here and taking all the jobs. This is a Britain which we recognize immediately, because it is so similar to our own. And, just like Britain today, the nation at that time was in the grip of an information revolution which was having a profound effect upon every aspect of life; including views on immigration. Fifty years earlier, it is doubtful if any working person would even have heard about the questions being asked in Parliament of the Home Secretary.

In the summer of 1911, the Edwardian information revolution was manifested chiefly in the almost universal reading by working-class people of cheap and readily-available newspapers; something which had only been a feature of life for a few years. Daily newspapers illustrated with photographs began circulating in 1904. Seeing moving pictures of current events was also something of a novelty in 1911, although it was starting to become an accepted part of life, chiefly for working-class people. These two media worked inadvertently together in August 1911 to produce a shocking phenomenon which had not been seen in Britain since the Middle Ages, namely anti-Jewish pogroms.

There had been serious rioting in South Wales in August 1911, connected with the industrial action on the railways and this had resulted in six deaths at Llanelli; two men shot dead by the army and four killed in a subsequent explosion during the looting of railway wagons. It was the hottest summer on record and hot, sunny weather is always a bad sign for the maintenance of public order. Even though the strike had now ended, the poorer people in the mining districts still had many grievances. These related to housing, lack of money and the fear of unemployment. The newsreel films and newspaper reports of things such as the Siege of Sidney Street and the supposed rise in cheap labour coming from abroad, men who might work for lower wages and therefore jeopardize the jobs of British workers, suggested another focus for their discontent. It must be the foreigners and Jews who were to blame for at least some of their problems! There were very few Jews living in South Wales at that time and the idea that the shopkeepers and owners of small businesses might really be responsible for any of the difficulties being faced in towns such as Tredegar and Ebbw Vale was ludicrous. The mining town of Tredegar, for instance, had a population of 20,000 and just thirty

Jewish families lived there. Nevertheless, they provided a handy and easily identifiable target. As we saw earlier, newspapers had been talking of 'Jews and foreigners', almost as though the two expressions were interchangeable. There were no foreigners in South Wales and so those angry about various issues would have to make do with the Jews.

On the night of Saturday, 19 August 1911, a series of concerted attacks were launched against the premises of Jews living in Tredegar and Ebbw Vale. There was widespread looting and many shops were wrecked; the damage including the removal of floorboards and light fittings. Families were driven from the district. The police were overwhelmed by the crowds, which some observers suggested were 10,000 strong and consisted of both men and women.

The rioting grew worse and by Monday, two magistrates in Ebbw Vale read the Riot Act and then appealed for help from the army to restore order. Troops, both infantry and cavalry, were despatched to Ebbw Vale. The infantry fixed bayonets and charged the crowd. At Brynmawr, cavalry cleared the streets and on the same night, a detachment of cavalry at Ebbw Vale drew their swords and cleared the streets by force. The same thing happened at Tredegar and other towns in the area. The Somerset Light Infantry and the Royal Warwickshire Regiment were kept very busy for the next few days.

There is no doubt that working people were having a tough time of it in the years following Queen Victoria's death and that they had legitimate worries about rising prices and falling wages. This had happened before, but in those days there had been no popular press or newsreels to point people in a certain direction and provide a convenient scapegoat. All the talk about foreigners and Jews being to blame for flooding the country with cheap labour, a common theme in some quarters, exacerbated the situation and precipitated anti-Jewish pogroms. Even the straightforward reporting of Parliamentary debates in which the number of foreigners entering the country each year was mentioned, served to stir up anger against outsiders.

Between 1901 and 1914, working-class people in Britain began to acquire a sense of themselves and a realisation that they were a power in the land. Looking at the nineteenth century, we find to our surprise that almost everything we know, or think that we know about working-class life is mediated via middle-class writers. The archetypal working-class youth of Victorian Britain must surely be the Artful Dodger, the fictional creation of a middle-class author. Much of what we know about the lives of ordinary people at that time comes from people like journalist Henry Mayhew, author of *London Labour and the London Poor*. Mayhew is one of the chief sources for what we know, or think we know, about working-class life in Victorian Britain. This means, to put it bluntly, that our knowledge of the lives of most people in Britain is meagre. By the time that Edward VII was on the throne though, 'the poor' had found a voice of their own.

Little writing by poor people themselves in nineteenth century Britain has survived. They were often illiterate and could not afford to buy paper, envelopes and stamps; so letters are rare. Ordinary people did not buy or read newspapers such as the *Times* or *Daily Telegraph*, so their views are not to be found there either. Photography was expensive, so the only working-class people recorded in this way are those whom middle-class photographers found sufficiently picturesque or eye-catching to be worth capturing on a glass plate, the occasional mudlark or street urchin perhaps. There are no films of them, very few diaries; in fact, the working class has left very little from that time.

How very different was the situation in Edwardian Britain! We know a huge amount about working-class people who then, as in Victorian times, made up the great majority of the population, from many different sources, including their own words. What did workers look like during the first years of the twentieth century? We have plenty of films of them, showing them leaving factories, working on farms or enjoying a day at the seaside. Some of these films are even in colour, like the 1908 film *A Visit to the Seaside*, which was filmed using a new process called Kinemacolour. In addition to this, the arrival of cheap cameras such as the Box Brownie in 1900 meant that working people could now afford to photograph their families and friends. The craze for 'selfies' began at this time, with people photographing themselves in the mirror! The introduction of the halftone method of reproducing photographs meant that newspapers and magazines were now able to feature visual images of ordinary life in their pages.

In print too, ordinary men and women were now able to set out accounts of their lives in a way which had been impossible before that time. Improvements in printing machinery, things like the Linotype machine, meant that newspapers and magazines were now cheap enough for most people to be able to afford them; the average cost for a weekly paper was one penny. Because of the burgeoning market, many of the new publications were aimed at specific groups of working men and women. For instance, 1903 saw the arrival of *The Wheel of Fortune; The Romance of Luck in Real Life, The Clean Slate; A Weekly Paper for Sportsmen and Playgoers* and *Competitions*, which contained 'Prizes, Thrilling Stories, Humour'. The following years saw the first editions of *Fortune,* with '10,000 Prizes for our readers', *The Winning Post* and *London Opinion.*

Weekly magazines and newspapers, together with the new daily papers like the *Daily Mirror* and *Daily Sketch*, allowed working people to express their views publicly. They wrote letters to the papers, something which would have been unheard-of fifty years earlier. These publications were for them. Reading them now, we can see what the interests and preoccupations of ordinary people were at that time.

Another, and perhaps even more significant, landmark was reached just before the outbreak of war in 1914. That was the year which saw the publication of the first British novel about working-class life which was actually written by a working man. *The Ragged-Trousered Philanthropists* shows what life was really like for those struggling somehow to survive on the lowest stratum of Edwardian society. For the first time, the authentic voice of an urban, working-class novelist was available.

Another way that the previously unheard masses left a tangible record for us to see today was in the form of postcards. New printing techniques meant that these were colourful and bright, costing only a halfpenny to send. Hundreds of millions of these were sent; over 850 million in 1908 alone. They were the equivalent of today's emails and texts and by reading the messages on them, we can build up a picture of the language being used by people in their dealings with family and friends.

All this means that the Edwardian world is accessible to us in a way that the lives of ordinary people in nineteenth-century Britain are not. This state of affairs was a direct result of developments in analogue technology which made possible the exponential growth of newspapers, magazines and cinema, and also laid the foundations for the third of the mass media which would come to dominate the first half of the century, that is to say radio.

Before looking in detail at how newspapers, cinema and, to a lesser extent, radio affected so greatly the day-to-day life of most people living in Britain in the years between 1901 and 1914, perhaps we might look in general at the nature of information revolutions. We are currently going through such a revolution, as did those living a little over a century ago, but these are not the only information revolutions that the world has known. There have been at least four previous ones before our Digital Revolution and each has changed the world forever.

Chapter 2

Information Revolutions and How They Change the World

The so-called Digital Revolution is also known sometimes as the Information Revolution, as a way of comparing and contrasting the changing nature of the modern world economy with that of the Industrial Revolution which preceded it. It would be more accurate to describe the current state of affairs as *an* information revolution, for it is just one of the revolutions in the recording and communication of information which have taken place. Indeed, the very history of the human race depends upon the first of these revolutions; that which saw the invention of writing. Without the permanent recording of events by those writing at the time, there can, by definition, be no history. This is of course why we describe that part of the human story which took place before writing as being 'prehistoric'.

Something which is not immediately apparent is that progress in information storage and methods of communication is not a smooth and continuous process, but rather happens in fits and starts. There are long plateaux when everything continues with little change for decades or centuries and then another explosion of innovation occurs, before everything settles down again and people get used to the new technology. We are of course in the middle of just such a period of change, which makes it hard to be objective about this subject. The latest information revolution has now been going on for over thirty years and it is not at all clear when it will end and we shall find ourselves going through another long stretch where nothing much is likely to happen in the field for a century or two. Nevertheless, history teaches us that just such a period will soon be upon us and the time will come when the frantic pace of change in our mobiles, computers, televisions and so on will slow down and indeed virtually come to a halt.

There have been at least four previous information revolutions before the present one. All have caused profound and irreversible changes to the societies in which they took place. Each successive episode of this kind affected more people than the one before, until we reach the present and latest of these waves of innovation and change in the handling of information, which has affected almost every single person in the developed world. In this book, we shall be looking at the fourth of these information revolutions, but it might be helpful first to place the Edwardian Analogue Revolution in context by seeing briefly what happened during the three earlier such episodes in history.

Humanity's first major development in the storage of information somewhere other than in the depths of the human brain took place in the Middle East, a little over 5,000 years ago, when merchants and traders began impressing marks into damp clay to indicate the type and quantity of goods which they were sending to other villages or towns. These early accounts evolved into the wedge-shaped marks which are known today as cuneiform. In the following centuries, the Egyptians began to use hieroglyphs and the Chinese developed their own system of writing, using pictograms. Perhaps the most significant by-product of this new method of recording information in permanent form was civilization itself.

Used in the first instance for keeping track of commercial transactions, the art of writing was soon adopted by the rulers of towns for their edicts, treaties, laws and religious pronouncements. The memories of men and women are fallible and prone to forgetfulness and error. When a set of laws, such as the famous code of Hammurabi, was chiselled into a monolith, they were, quite literally, set in stone. More than that, there could no longer be any dispute about those laws; they were in a sense public property. The Code of Hammurabi may be seen in Illustration 4. It was no longer necessary when some legal point was challenged to hunt out an old man and probe his, perhaps failing, memory. The information was stored so effectively that 4,000 years later, we are still able to consult the ancient king of Babylon's code of laws. Only when laws, rules and agreements are recorded permanently in this way can there be any prospect of stable civil society.

Once writing appeared, then governments emerged which controlled not merely one city and its surrounding territory, but groups of cities and towns. This in turn led first to the rise of nations and then of empires. Not until a ruler could communicate his unequivocal wishes to subjects hundreds of miles away was it possible for civilizations to arise. The king's seal on a written document guaranteed its authenticity and ensured that orders were clearly understood.

A point to bear in mind, and we shall see later its relevance, is that to begin with writing was a specialized art. It was not used in general by the common people but was rather the province of trained scribes and their patrons, usually kings, priests or civil servants. However much written material was produced, and whatever the medium used, the great majority of people throughout the ages would have been unable either to read or write. This set a natural limit upon actual access to the information stored on clay tablets and papyrus.

The next big step in the storage of data was the invention of movable type for printing, which took place in fifteenth-century Europe. Instead of all copies of every book having to be laboriously written by hand, it now became possible to mass-produce books, pamphlets, sermons and political tracts. An almost immediate consequence of this new method of transmitting and storing knowledge was that Europe was plunged into the upheaval which we know as the Reformation.

In the middle of the fifteenth century Johannes Gutenberg set up a printing press in the German town of Mainz. He could not have realized it, but in doing so he was in effect ushering in the modern age. For over a thousand years, the Catholic Church had had a virtual monopoly in Europe on the dissemination of philosophy and ideas. Of course, heretics and rebels cropped up from time to time, but with no way of spreading their heterodox notions widely, other than by word of mouth, it had always been fairly easy for the Church to suppress such men and women by burning their bodies and persecuting their followers. This was to change dramatically with the invention of the printing press. The kind of printing press used by Gutenberg may be seen in Illustration 5. It is possible to print only one page at a time on a machine of this sort, but even so, this is infinitely faster than copying manuscripts by hand.

In 1517 Martin Luther, who was Professor of Moral Theology at the University of Wittenberg, disagreed with the Church on the question of papal indulgences. Briefly, this was a racket operated by the Catholic Church whereby people who had died could have their punishment in the afterlife remitted by a cash payment given by the grieving relatives to Rome. Luther wrote ninety-five theses which explained why this practice was unacceptable. This sort of thing had happened before, without its affecting anybody much, chiefly because few people heard about such disputes. This time though, Martin Luther's arguments were printed as a pamphlet and circulated throughout Germany. A priest who was opposed to Luther wrote a counter-argument, which was also printed. It was the fact that radical ideas could now be spread rapidly in printed material which meant that it was impossible for the Church to stifle this new teaching. Within a few decades, Europe had split into the northern Protestant states and the southern

Catholic ones. This upheaval had been precipitated almost entirely by the creation of a new medium.

Two things should be mentioned at this point, which are true of all information revolutions, from the invention of writing to the rise of the Internet. The first is that whatever way information is stored or knowledge spread, there is no guarantee that what you read or see is accurate and true. This is the case today when looking at Internet sites; but it was equally true of cuneiform inscriptions and medieval pamphlets. Just as men and women lie verbally, so too are they liable to do so when writing, taking photographs or making films. The ancient stele upon which the laws of Hammurabi are inscribed describes him as 'King of the four quarters of the world', which was something of an exaggeration. There exist contradictory accounts from antiquity in which two kings would both claim to have been the victors in some battle. With the arrival of writing, propaganda and fake news began to be fixed for all time and for future generations to see. Writing may record falsehood as easily as it does truth! Moving forward a little to the Edwardian period, the new medium of moving pictures was being used to deceive viewers almost from the beginning. Today, we know about photo-shopping of images and the way in which this can create false impressions; but there is nothing new about such impostures. During the Russo-Japanese War of 1905, there was a demand for newsreel film and so some enterprising companies filmed re-enactments of both land battles and naval engagements and tried to pass them off as the real thing. This sort of thing has happened throughout history with every new means of conveying news or recording information.

Another common feature of each successive information revolution is the way in which innovative methods of handling information are soon exploited for uses which governments and religious leaders denounce as frivolous, dangerous or immoral. We know that the Internet is at least as full of pornography and fake news as it is of objective and useful knowledge. It is also suggested today that this relatively new means of exchanging information and communicating with others, which we call the Internet or World Wide Web, might somehow be harmful to children. This too is an old idea when something new crops up, and printing was no exception. When printing was introduced into England by William Caxton, the first books he produced were worthy works of classical or religious interest. It did not take long though before more entertaining stories were being printed and published; a lot of which was designed to appeal to younger readers. Take *The Friar and the Boy* for example, in which a young boy acquires a charm which causes his cruel stepmother to fart uncontrollably. The story is told in rhyme and was published in the early sixteenth century as a pamphlet. After the stepmother farts in front of her family and friends, the story ends with the lines:

> Fie said the Boy unto his Dame
> Temper thy telltale bum for shame.

This was doubtless very amusing stuff for Tudor teenagers, but it led to accusations that the new medium of printing was corrupting young people.

William Tyndale, who translated the Bible into English, was very worried about the effect that printed material was having upon children and young people. It was one thing when this new technology enabled them to have access to prayer books or the works of Euclid, but this wasn't all that they were looking at! In 1528 Tyndale could remain silent no longer on this subject. He wrote that the printed pamphlets to which young people had free access contained a lot of unsuitable stuff, things such as:

> Robin Hood and Bevis of Hampton, Hercules, Hector and Troylus, with a thousand histories and fables of love and wantons and of ribaldry, as filthy as heart can think, to corrupt the minds of youth withal.

From the modern perspective, such a complaint seems incredible. Imagine parents today moaning because their children are spending too much of their time reading tales from Greek mythology!

The Industrial Revolution, which began in Britain before spreading to continental Europe, marked the onset of the next stage in what might be termed the democratisation of information. Working on the assumption that knowledge is power, the British government had been fighting to prevent the general population from having access to up-to-the-minute information about everything and anything, from Parliamentary debates to world affairs and new political ideas. This had been done by various means; ranging from laws which made it a criminal offence to spread rumours to the outright banning of newspapers. By the eighteenth century, slightly more subtle and indirect means were being employed. One of these was the Stamp Act, which increased the price of newspapers to well beyond what the average working man might reasonably be able to afford.

First introduced in 1712, the Stamp Act imposed a hefty tax on every copy of newspapers. It was later combined with taxes on paper and also the advertisements which newspapers needed to survive. The result was that newspapers increased in price until they were beyond the means of most people. This set a natural limit upon the spread of knowledge and information about current affairs during the eighteenth and early nineteenth centuries, a situation which continued in Britain until July 1855, when Stamp Duty was abolished. That same year saw the publication of the *Daily Telegraph*, the first newspaper in Britain to sell for just 1d (less than half of 1p in modern currency). With the end of duty on paper six years later, the age of the cheap newspaper had definitely arrived.

The abolition of Stamp Duty and the tax on paper were part of the third information revolution, the one which preceded that which took place during the Edwardian period. This third information revolution saw the development of new methods for printing, which had an especially great effect upon the production of newspapers.

The chief distinguishing feature of information revolutions is that they see information being made accessible to greater numbers of people as a result of new inventions or radical innovations to old inventions. The invention of printing with moveable type in the fifteenth century allowed pamphlets and books to be produced far more rapidly than when such things were laboriously copied out by hand. The distribution of information was still limited though by the literacy of the general population. However many books are circulating in a society, the knowledge which they contain will have little influence on society unless there are enough people who are able to read them. Much the same applies to newspapers as well. In 1814, the *Times* had a print run of only 4,500 copies a day. This was because it was both very expensive and also because fewer than half the adults in the country were able to read.

The information revolution which coincided with the latter part of the Industrial Revolution in Britain had several causes. On the one hand, new methods were developed for printing newspapers, which made it easier to produce large numbers of them and reduced costs by making it possible to run the printing presses with fewer workers. Just before the end of the Napoleonic Wars, two Germans living in Britain devised a new kind of printing press, one which would mechanize the process and allow it to be operated by steam power. From 1810 onwards, Friedrich Koenig and Andreas Bauer patented designs for steam-driven printing presses. The first edition of the *Times* to be produced in this way on the new cylinder press was that of

29 November 1814. It was, in retrospect, the most significant development in printing since the time of Gutenberg. The steam rotary press installed at the *Times* may be seen in Illustration 6.

Twenty years after the revolution in printing technology came the electric telegraph, which enabled information and news to be transmitted at the speed of light. Contemporaneously with these inventions came a steep rise in the literacy rate in Britain, which meant of course a greater market for printed material of kind. By the end of the nineteenth century, over 90 per cent of adults could read and with the end of the 'taxes on knowledge', the demand for newspapers and books as the new century approached was unprecedented.

There is always a risk when thinking about past times that we will fall into the trap of believing that people were different a hundred or a thousand years ago, that they were more virtuous, serious-minded or industrious, for example. When we look at old photographs of the Victorians, it is difficult to imagine that they were as fond of pornography as we in the twenty-first century and that just as we use the most up-to-date technology to create and consume images of naked men and women, so too did they. Unless we realize that the Edwardians were people very much like us, with the same tendencies and desires, it will be difficult to understand the way that their wishes directed the development of information and communication technology between the death of Queen Victoria and the beginning of the First World War. Perhaps looking at how this kind of thing happened over the last decade or two of our own time will make this a little clearer.

From 1990 onwards, the expression 'Information Superhighway' was increasingly bandied about. The idea then was that networks of fibre-optic cables would eventually link every citizen to a vast number of computers which would be able to supply them with all the knowledge in the world. This would create a new society, where businesses, government departments and of course individuals would have unparalleled access to information. It was a worthy vision, which has largely come to pass. However, it is the ways in which this 'Information Superhighway' is actually used which nobody twenty or thirty years ago could have foreseen. Who would have guessed in 1990 that teenagers would be more likely to be sending photographs of their genitals along the Information Superhighway than to be researching algebra for their homework? Did anybody foresee that viewing clips of films showing kittens on skateboards would be a huge attraction of this fantastic new means of exchanging information, or that pornography would be one of its major and enduring features? It is probably fair to say that none of those talking with so much eager anticipation about the Information Superhighway gave much thought to any of these possibilities!

The uses to which new methods of gathering and spreading information will actually be used are seldom obvious in advance. This is odd, because we only need to study history a little to see what has happened repeatedly. When printing became a big thing in England, everybody assumed as a matter of course that it would be a tremendously good way of producing Bibles and works of mathematics and philosophy. What was less apparent to those enthusiastically championing the new medium was that in next to no time, people would be using it to turn out dirty poems and lurid accounts of the sex lives of the ancient Greeks. This happened of course because those were the sort of things that people really *wanted*.

There is a general principle at work here, one which explains both how the Internet has come to be used in the way that it so often is and also the reason that the Hollywood film industry came into being. It can most clearly be seen at work in the Edwardian period, when various new media such as radio and moving pictures became popular. It is a universal principle; as applicable to Victorian England as it is to the world of the twenty-first century. Lord Reith, the first Director-General of the BBC, famously claimed that he saw his mission as enriching people's lives by radio programmes which would inform, educate and entertain them. The order in which he placed those three words suggests the priority which he placed upon the three aims; first to inform and educate and only then to entertain. Reith did not pluck those notions of what a new medium should strive towards from thin air. They sum up what all educated and influential men and women suppose should be the role of all media, whether printing, recorded sound, moving pictures, wireless telegraphy or the Internet. It is this mentality which the Edwardian man and woman in the street rebelled against, and in doing so helped shape the world as we know it today.

Before seeing the way in which this attitude shaped the development of the new media in Edwardian Britain, we will look back to the previous century and consider two innovations then which promised initially to be of great educational value and how they were eventually used. At the Great Exhibition, held at Hyde Park in 1851, stereoscopic photographs were displayed. These were made by taking two photographs a little distance apart and then viewing them through a special device with separate lenses for each eye, forming a three-dimensional image. The modern-day Viewmaster works on the same principle.

Queen Victoria herself was hugely impressed with the stereoscopic photographs and a viewer was ordered to be sent to Buckingham Palace.

This began a craze for stereoscopy; it had received the royal seal of approval. The idea was that far-off places could be seen by those who could not travel to see them in real life. Scenes of the Lake District, the pyramids in Egypt and a hundred other locations were photographed in this way. The whole purpose was elevated and serious; to allow people to explore foreign countries from the comfort of their parlour. Of course, this was all well and good, but it didn't take long for other demands to made upon this novel type of photography. Specifically, it became used for a great deal of very explicit pornography which proved far more popular than views of Indian village life or the Great Wall of China. The stereoscope as educational device had become no more than a form of vulgar entertainment.

Illustration 7 shows a very early example of the way in which stereoscopic photographs were used for pornographic purposes. It is a glass Daguerreotype, dating from the 1850s. This image is not only three-dimensional, it is also in colour! The young woman exposing her breasts has been delicately painted by hand, using a French process in which the pigments were fixed by using transparent gum. The end-product, when viewed through the necessary apparatus, is stunningly realistic. There is no invention, from stereoscopy to the World Wide Web, which cannot be exploited for titillation of this kind.

An even more interesting case is that of the phonograph invented by Thomas Edison; the ancestor of the disc-playing gramophone. A few months after perfecting his machine, which played cylinders wrapped in tin foil, rather than the more familiar flat records, an article appeared in the magazine *North American Review*. In an edition of June 1878, Edison predicted some of the uses to which his new invention might be put in the future. In hindsight, these make amusing reading. He listed:

1. Letter writing and all kinds of dictation without the aid of a stenographer.
2. Phonographic books, which will speak to blind people without effort on their part.
3. The teaching of elocution.
4. The reproduction of music.
5. The 'Family Record' – a registry of sayings, reminiscences etc. by members of the family in their own voices, and the last words of the dying.
6. Music-boxes and toys.
7. Clocks that should announce in articulate speech the time for going home, going to meals etc.

8. The preservation of languages by exact reproduction of the manner of pronouncing.

9. Educational purposes; such as preserving the explanations made by a teacher, so that the pupil can refer to them at any moment, and spelling or other lessons place on the phonograph for convenience in committing to memory.

10. Connection with the telephone, so as to make that instrument an auxiliary in the transmission of permanent and invaluable records, instead of being the recipient of momentary and fleeting communications.

It will at once be seen that the chief purposes for which its inventor intended the permanent recording of sound were serious and high-minded; it was to educate and inform, rather than entertain. True, the reproduction of music is referred to, but this was almost in passing. Strangely enough, when the public took to phonographs, and their successors gramophones, they showed no inclination to use them for recording the sayings and reminiscences of their elderly relatives. They wanted to use them almost exclusively as a means of entertainment. Music and songs were what were wanted and it is for this that we remember the gramophone and record player. They may indeed have been used by ethnologists for recording the speech patterns of remote tribes, as Thomas Edison suggested, but this was by no means the use to which they were generally put; still less were they telling people when to go home or eat their dinner!

In fact, one of the earliest mentions that we have of the professional use of phonographs in the 1880s was not for books for the blind, worthwhile though such a use would have been. Rather, phonographs were being used in high-class brothels, where patrons could listen to obscene ditties and even record themselves using the kind of language which no well-bred Victorian gentleman would be likely to use in the family home.

The stereoscope and the phonograph indicate what was to be expected of moving pictures and wireless telegraphy when they came along, that well-meaning and well-educated people would hope earnestly that these new ways of communicating with others and storing information would primarily be used for educational purposes and the broadening of minds. We might also expect to see ordinary people preferring to use such things for sheer entertainment. Which is of course just what happened. Some of the earliest moving pictures, which appeared just before the beginning of the twentieth century, were exhibited in the peepshows called 'Mutoscopes'.

Not for nothing did these come to be known in Britain as 'What the butler saw' machines.

Two ideas have been sketched out in this chapter. The first is that each new information revolution has increased the amount of information available and also seen it reaching a greater proportion of the population. Today, this tendency has seen almost every home in the country having access to literally unlimited information via the Internet. The Edwardian information revolution, fuelled by analogue technology, was very similar to this; ensuring that a very high percentage of people in Britain were provided with access to printed text, photographs and moving images of the world beyond their own, often narrow and restricted, lives. It was an opening up of perspectives; a new way of seeing what lay beyond their own horizons.

Hand-in-hand with increasing access to facts and figures, we will see another tendency, which is that people often do not wish for new technology to educate and inform them; they wish rather to be amused and entertained by it. By 1904, many working men and women could afford to buy The *Times*, had they wished to do so, but they preferred to purchase the *Daily Mirror*, with its photographs of actresses and lurid accounts of sensational murders. There was little appetite for ploughing through Parliamentary debates, but a huge desire to read about the scandalous private lives of famous people. For many of those who could now afford a daily newspaper, their primary aim was to be entertained. How these tastes were catered for by men such as Alfred Harmsworth will be the subject of the next chapter. Before we turn to this though, perhaps we should consider another point about information revolutions, which is that they tend to make older people feel a little uneasy; as though they are being left behind.

Of course, middle-aged people don't generally want to admit that they are having trouble keeping up with the modern world, lest it make them appear like old fogies! Instead, they can object to new information technology on the grounds that it is harming children and young people. Expressing such concerns make older people feel responsible and altruistic, rather than as though they are exposing themselves to ridicule by being unable to keep abreast of the rapidly-changing nature of the modern world. In our own time, we see this phenomenon very clearly. Young people adapt easily to the changing face of the Internet; not so their parents! Ten years ago, we were communicating via emails and Internet chat rooms. Then came Facebook and now it is all Snapchat and Instagram. Youngsters have no difficulty following these changes, but many older people find it bewildering. They display their frustration at such aspects of the information revolution in which we are now living by claiming that children are being harmed, or at the very least, put at risk by these new developments. This too is a recurring feature of information revolutions.

For the Tudors, it was printing which was allowing young people to encounter unsuitable material. In the nineteenth century, novels were a hazard, particularly to girls. Reading novels made them lazy and excited them sexually. These days, of course, it is the sharing of indecent images electronically which exercises the minds of parents and other adults. Demands are made to restrict or even prevent the use of technology for such purposes. Not only that, but the Internet, especially that part of it known as the 'Dark Web' is used by terrorists and subversives who are intent upon destroying our way of life. Then there is the fact that using the Internet has discouraged young people from reading books, another bad thing.

The Analogue Revolution which took place in the opening years of the twentieth century was marked by fears of the effects which it would have on certain parts of society. Children were being exposed to unsuitable material, the use of English was becoming slovenly and corrupted with abbreviations and slang, dangerous idea were being circulated with the aid of new technology and there was a boom in indecent images. Today, such fears focus almost exclusively upon the Internet, but at the time of the Edwardians, there were various new means of communication and so it will be best to deal with these individually. We shall begin by looking at the first, genuine mass medium, the popular newspapers which first made their appearance in the closing years of Victoria's reign, but which came into their own when her son became king.

Chapter 3

The Birth of the Mass Media – Newspapers

The first years of the twentieth century really saw the emergence of mass media as we understand the term today. This was part of the Analogue Revolution at which we have been looking and the tone set in those days has largely persisted through to the present. It may best be summarised by saying that most people see the role of the mass media as entertaining them; rather than feeding them information and facts.

Before looking in detail at this subject, it might be as well to remind ourselves what we mean by the expression 'mass media'. The *Oxford English Dictionary* defines a 'medium' as; 'a means by which something is communicated or expressed'. The plural of medium is of course media and so the mass media are simply the different ways that things are communicated to large numbers of people at the same time.

The first mass medium was the printed word. From the fifteenth century until about 1900, print was the only medium capable of reaching many people. Mass media are different from purely local media such as provincial newspapers and little radio stations serving just one city or district. To qualify as part of the mass media, a newspaper, television station or film maker really must reach the population of a whole country. From that perspective, national newspapers like The *Times* might be considered a mass medium in Britain during much of the nineteenth century, but this is a little misleading.

Throughout much of the nineteenth century, at least half the adults in Britain were unable to read and were therefore unlikely to be buying, or even looking at, newspapers. Because of the taxes, at which we shall be looking below, the price of newspapers was artificially high, meaning that few ordinary, working people could afford them. We shall see shortly how this all changed by the end of the century, but first we must look at the very idea of newspapers and see how they were once viewed by the authorities in Britain.

Living as we do in a world where mass-circulation newspapers are part of the established order, it is difficult to grasp just how revolutionary and radical the idea once was of printing and circulating information about what is going on in the world; especially touching upon events in one's own country. Today newspapers are, along with television and radio, referred to as the 'Mainstream Media', meaning that they represent the conventional and traditional way of distributing news. It was not always so. At one time, the very act of publishing a newspaper was regarded as seditious and calculated to damage the authority of the government. Simply relating what was happening politically and socially in the country was thought to be dangerous and undesirable. The publication of news was, in itself, felt to be an unwarranted interference in state affairs.

There is of course no such thing as unbiased news. This can be clearly observed when looking at two of the first English newspapers which were published during the English Civil War. Even when somebody can manage to keep his or her own views and opinions out of the way when writing a newspaper report, there will be a bias in what news is written about or reported. The news which we select says a lot about our own personal prejudices. This will be the case even if the editorial policy is one of strict neutrality. Although there was, until the seventeenth century, government disapproval of printing information about domestic affairs, newspapers covering foreign news were tolerated, at least up to a point. So, in the 1620s, a paper was circulating in London called *Courante or Weekly Newes from Italy, Germany, Hungarie, Spaine and France.* Several papers of this sort were distributed in London until 1632, until an item in one of them upset both the Spanish and Austrian ambassadors. The Court of the Star Chamber, which was responsible for state security, then banned all newspapers. This prohibition was relaxed in 1638, and the publication of domestic political news was, for the first time, permitted in England.

When the English Civil War began a few years after the newspapers reporting English affairs first appeared, it was at once seen why the authorities had been so hesitant in the past about letting newspapers of this kind exist. Two of the earliest such sources of news were both virulently partisan and saw it as their duty to champion one side or another in the struggle between Parliament and the King, rather than impartially reporting what was going on in the country. John Birkenhead, for example, founded the *Mercurious Aulicus.* According to the masthead, this contained, 'Truth impartially related from thence to the whole kingdom'. The game was given away by the fact that above the title of the newspaper were large engravings of the King and Queen. For the opposing side, the *Diurnalls* set out the Roundhead point of view. Rather than reporting news, these newspapers were really agitating on behalf of Parliament or

King. This was their chief purpose; rather than just informing readers what was happening.

By the beginning of the eighteenth century, newspapers were appearing across much of Britain, but many were less concerned with distributing news that they were in attacking government policy and, as those running the country thought, creating mischief. It was no longer possible or politically desirable to suppress such things simply by passing a law and banning them, so the idea was dreamed up of taxing them out of existence. In 1712, the Stamp Act was passed; with the specific aim of restricting the flow of information to the public. Newspapers were now taxed at 1d a page. Other publications were also covered by the act, including political pamphlets.

As a consequence of the Paper Tax and Stamp Tax, the *Times* in 1815 cost 6d, between 2p and 3p in modern currency. Two-thirds of this price was to cover the tax payable on each copy of a newspaper at that time. The aim of this tax, which has been described as a 'tax on knowledge', was no secret; it was to prevent ordinary men and women from being able to afford newspapers. The British government believed that cheap newspapers had inflamed the situation in America, helping to fan the flames of the revolution there. They also felt that the French Revolution had been caused in part by the circulation of dangerous new ideas. The hope was that by preventing these ideas from being printed and distributed to the working classes, the danger of any kind of uprising in Britain could be averted. There was, it was true, popular unrest, but this was not always articulated by those dissatisfied with their lot. It was therefore thought necessary to suppress cheap publications, lest they encourage radical and seditious ideologies to flourish. Speaking in 1819, of the Newspapers Stamp Duty Act, Lord Ellenborough explained that 'It was not against the respectable press that this Bill was directed, but against the pauper press.'

In many ways, the tax on newspapers achieved its end. By raising the cost of newspapers to 6d or 7d, they became beyond the reach of most working people. In 1815, an agricultural labourer might expect to earn perhaps two shillings (10p) a day. This meant that buying a copy of the *Times* every day would have taken about a quarter of a working man's income. Clearly, this medium, although technically nationwide, was unlikely to reach everybody! It cannot really be called a mass medium at all. If we now fast-forward ninety years, to the time when Edward VII was on the throne, matters were completely different. By then, the price of the new, popular newspapers such as the *Daily Mail* and *Daily Mirror* had fallen to a halfpenny, about a quarter of 1p, while a labourer's wages had risen to over five shillings a day

(25p). In short, a daily paper now cost not a quarter of a working-class man or woman's salary but less than one per cent.

Newspaper stamp duty was finally abolished in 1855, at which point it became possible to sell newspapers at a lower price. Despite this, it took another forty years before mass-circulation papers appeared in Britain. The popular press came into being during Edward VII's reign in part because this was the first time in the country's history that almost everybody could read and write. The number of people who might buy the new newspapers was limited only by the actual population of Britain. This was a strange situation and one which was quite unprecedented. Literacy had always in the past been a minority attribute. In Shakespeare's time, when printing was beginning to flourish in Britain, only about one child in eight attended school. This tended to set a natural and very low limit on the number of literate people in the country. Since it was only those able to read and write who would be in the market for books and other printed material, this in turn made printing an activity which catered for a minority; those who had been educated. Because schools were all fee-paying at that time, those who read printed matter were usually the better-off.

As the centuries passed, more and more children received some kind of education, however rudimentary. The rise of literacy was a slow process though and by the time that Victoria ascended the throne in 1838, half of all British adults were still unable to read or write. We know this by the number of couples who signed the register when they got married, not with their names but by making a mark such as a cross. In 1840, a third of men were still signing their names in this way, as well as half the women getting married. There would obviously be no point in producing popular newspapers aimed at such individuals.

All this changed in 1870, when a law was passed which provided for education for all children in Britain, from the age of five. Ten years later, school attendance was made compulsory and as a result, illiteracy was virtually abolished over the next twenty years or so. Looking at the marriage registers for 1900 shows us that over 97 per cent of those getting married were now able to sign their names. This, then, was the situation as the twentieth century began. A new generation of young adults were almost all literate and starting to read for pleasure. Other factors were at work which allowed newspapers to become the first mass medium in the twentieth century. One of these was that an increasing number of working men and women now had available time in which they could read newspapers.

In the first half of the nineteenth century, there was no public transport in Britain, other than stage coaches and a few cabs plying for hire in the cities. These means of travel were too expensive for most people to think of using regularly and so the majority of workers lived as near to their place of work as possible and walked there and back each day. Hours of work were long and sometimes there was a long walk to get there as well, all of which meant that most working-class people had little leisure time. In the second half of the century, this changed. With the advent of nationwide railways and underground trains in London, the middle classes took to commuting – living in the suburbs and working in the centre of cities. At first, this lifestyle was too expensive for working-class people, but in 1883 Parliament passed the Cheap Trains Act, which meant that railway companies were obliged to run early morning and late evening trains to and from city centres at just 1d a journey. This made commuting an affordable lifestyle for everybody and with the building of tramways in the industrial areas of the country as well, it became possible for working people to move from the crowded slums near their places of work in the heart of the cities and to move out to suburbs. As a direct consequence, these new, working-class commuters were spending an hour or two each day travelling by train, tram or bus.

By the end of the century, it was noticed that reading while commuting had become an established pastime among all classes. W.H. Smith's shops catered for this trend by selling cheap novels and even opening their own lending library, where for 1d one could borrow a book from one branch of Smith's and return it to another. There can be no doubt that with the dawn of the new century, the time was right for some enterprising businessman to start catering for this mass market by producing newspapers which working men and women would want to read on their way to work in the morning.

Two technical developments in the late nineteenth century made it possible to exploit this new market more effectively. Both related to printing. From the time of Gutenberg's first printing press in the fifteenth century, until a decade or two before the dawn of the twentieth century, printing was a matter of selecting individual pieces of type and setting them into a frame. To print the word 'cat', it would have been necessary to take a piece of print for the letter 'C' and then place it in position. The process would be repeated for 'A' and 'T'. This was a fiddly, skilled and time-consuming enterprise. In 1884, a German-born inventor called Ottmar Merganthaler, who lived in the United States, patented a new method for printing, one which speeded up the process six-fold and did away with the need for skilled printers to select each piece of type by hand.

The Linotype machine which Merganthaler devised produced an entire line of print to use, instead of laboriously placing every single letter into place. It did this by arranging not print, but moulds. A ninety-character keyboard allowed the operator to release brass moulds for letters and line them up automatically. These brass moulds were held in magazines until needed. When an entire line of moulds had been arranged in this way, molten metal was poured in and the line of print was, as soon as it had cooled, ready to use. A supply of the molten alloy, a mixture of lead and antimony, was kept heated and ready for use and the completed line of type was cooled by water. This accounts for the other term by which the Linotype was known; hot metal typesetting.

Illustration 8 shows a Linotype keyboard and it can be seen at once that typing text on such a machine could not fail to be faster than fiddling around with little letters and pushing them into place. The Linotype, so-called of course because it prepared a whole 'line o' type' at a time, revolutionized the production of newspapers by both speeding up the entire enterprise and also cutting costs dramatically by dispensing with the need for employing many highly-skilled men to handle and manipulate individual letters and form them into words. Obviously, speedy printing which could be undertaken by relatively unskilled workers was a boon for the newspaper industry. It enabled the production of newspapers in the Edwardian period which sold for only a halfpenny; less than a quarter of 1p.

The second of the inventions which brought about the revolution in the wider circulation and reading of newspapers at that time was the ability to print photographs easily. Some magazines in the nineteenth century had been illustrated with photographs, but these had been individually produced from a negative in the usual way and then simply glued to the page. There was no way to print them as swiftly as text could now be turned out with the aid of the Linotype machine.

There were one or two false starts, but the invention of a method to print photographs as easily as text proved to be the key to turning out newspapers which would sell in their hundreds of thousands or even millions across the whole nation. Traditional newspapers like the *Times* were aimed primarily at well-to-do men who needed to know what was going on politically and economically. Whole pages of dense print were devoted to verbatim accounts of long Parliamentary debates, in which every word of speeches on such abstruse topics as tariff reform was given. These subjects might have been of enormous importance to MPs, financiers and bankers, but were of little interest to the average worker. The front page of the *Times* was covered not, as is now the case, with photographs and the most important stories of the day, but rather with dozens of advertisements, a practice which continued until 1966. It lent the paper a dull and unattractive appearance. What if, instead of closely-printed pages of small print, it was possible to feature photographs? This would certainly liven up the appearance of the front page of a newspaper and make it more attractive to those who wanted a little human interest, rather than long lists of figures, statistics and government reports. This is where one of the analogue methods which had been developed in the last few decades of the nineteenth century came into its own.

The chief problem with printing pictures in newspapers up to the end of the nineteenth century was that by the very nature of printing; one could either print black ink on the paper or simply leave it white. Black-and-white photographs are of course made up in the main of varying shades of grey. It was portraying these half tones between black-and-white which had never been possible. Sometimes, photographs would be copied by an engraver and this version, made up of lines and dots, would be printed. The breakthrough came in the early 1870s and it occurred simultaneously in Sweden and the United States. The halftone process entailed breaking photographs down into a series of large and small dots. This was done by copying the image through a screen made up of lines or holes and then using this second image as the basis for the print. Dark areas were composed of many large dots and the lighter areas were made up of fewer and smaller dots. In this way, fine graduations of light and shade could be reproduced in black-and-white. Seen at a distance, large dots of black on white appear to be dark grey. Smaller or fewer dots give the illusion of light grey. In short, although only black-and-white are on the page, the human eye perceives these fields of dots as being shaded areas. A similar process is still used to this day in newspapers and examining a newspaper photograph closely will reveal that it is composed of many dots of primary colours which, viewed from a distance, give the illusion of any required shade.

At first, the new process was used only in specialist books and the occasional periodical. In Britain, the first halftone photographs to illustrate a magazine were of animals in London Zoo. These were featured in the *Graphic*, on 5 September 1885. For the next few years, such images cropped up in various periodicals, but were regarded as novelty items. Newspapers still consisted only of densely-packed text. The first newspaper regularly to use photographs of this type was Alfred Harmsworth's *Daily Mirror*.

Harmsworth, later to become Lord Northcliffe, had already had a great success with his *Daily Mail*, which began publication in 1896. This new paper cost only a halfpenny, half the price of other daily newspapers, and it was written in a livelier style than other papers being published in late Victorian Britain. As Harmsworth himself put it, 'four leading articles, a page of Parliament, and columns of speeches will NOT be found'. Not everybody approved of the content and form of the *Daily Mail,* which focused more upon human interest stories than it did Parliamentary debates. Lord Salisbury, Prime Minister between 1895 and 1902, dismissed it as being 'a newspaper produced by office boys for office boys'. Nevertheless, the *Daily Mail* was tremendously popular, the first print run being almost 400,000 copies. Within a short time, it had become the best-selling newspaper in Britain. If Lord Salisbury was contemptuous of the *Daily Mail,* it is difficult to know what he would have made of the *Daily Mirror,* which began publication a couple of months after his death!

Originally designed as a newspaper 'for gentlewomen', the first edition of the *Daily Mirror* came out on 2 November 1903. Its evolution over the next two years shows clearly the way in which technology, combined with the demands of the consumers, shaped the world we live in today. The first copy of the *Daily Mirror,* according to Alfred Harmsworth, was to be 'entertaining without being frivolous and serious without being dull'. A novel aspect of the new publication was that all the staff, from the editor Mary Howarth downwards, were women. It cost 1d; twice as much as the *Daily Mail.* Whether it succeeded in the stated aim of being entertaining and not dull, would be for readers to decide. Readers did not take at all to the *Daily Mirror* and the paper was such a flop that Harmsworth sacked all the female staff after two months and replaced them with men, re-launching the *Daily Mirror* on 26 January 1904 as the *Daily Illustrated Mirror,* halving its price at the same time.

The chief problem with the *Daily Mirror* had been that despite Harmsworth's assurances to the contrary, it *was* dull. The first issue had, like all serious newspapers at that time, advertisements on the front page. Turning to the second page, which contained the news, showed at once that this was not really a newspaper which was calculated to appeal to ordinary people. The greater part of the page beneath the masthead was taken up with the Court Circular, which informed readers that 'His Majesty the King received the Right Hon. Sir Francis Plunkett (His Majesty's Ambassador at Vienna) . . .'. It also contained such snippets as that His Serene Highness Prince Louis of Battenberg had visited the king the day before and that the Princess of Wales had attended divine service at the Marlborough House chapel. This sort of information might well have been the convention at the time, but it was never the less dull for all that! It was new technology which was to rescue the failing paper.

The *Daily Illustrated Mirror* was to be just that; that is to say that it would contain plenty of pictures. The front page was enlivened by engravings, but on the inside were to be found halftone photographs. This was not the first time that photographs had appeared in a British newspaper. As early as 4 November 1891, the *Daily Graphic* had printed a portrait of George Lambert, the Liberal candidate in a forthcoming election, but this had been a studio portrait. What made the *Daily Illustrated Mirror* different is that they employed their own staff photographers. The intention was not simply to feature portraits and 'studies', but to send their men out to obtain news photographs.

Even before it began to show photographs on the front page, which happened first on 22 March 1904, the *Daily Illustrated Mirror* was filling its front page with pictures. On 4 February 1904, for example, three-quarters of the front page was taken up with a portrait of Winston Churchill, who even then, ten years before the start of the First World War, was making his mark. The engraving which shows the absurdly young-looking Churchill bears the caption, 'Mr Winston Churchill gets his way'. Prime Minister Arthur Balfour had given the 29-year-old MP a minor post in government.

Now that photographs *could* be used in newspapers, it was inevitable that they *would*. The engravings which were the commonest type of pictures in magazines and newspapers at that time were beginning to look more than a little old-fashioned. Photography had, after all, been around for over seventy years and it was something of an anachronism that the same type of engravings and woodcuts were still being used as might have been seen in a newspaper from the eighteenth century.

When another newspaper designed to appeal to the ordinary man in the street appeared on 15 March 1909, its front page was covered with photographs from the very first issue. The *Daily Sketch* proclaimed beneath its masthead that it was, 'The all-picture morning paper'. The halftone process of printing photographs meant that any newspaper which hoped to achieve a large circulation would from now on have to be illustrated not with the occasional engraving but with as many real photographs as possible.

The Linotype machine and halftone photograph process had between them created the popular press as we know it today. It had also precipitated the rise of the newspaper magnate or press baron; the man in charge of a number of newspapers. Such characters, typified by Alfred Harmsworth and his brother Harold, later to become Viscount Northcliffe and Viscount

Rothermere respectively, came to exercise enormous influence on the affairs of the countries in which they operated. Of course, their original aim was nothing more than the acquisition of large amounts of money, but as the years passed, this proved not to be enough to satisfy them. They wanted power as well. Not only did they wish to report news, they also wanted to create it and ultimately to get governments to do their bidding. A few years after the end of the First World War, Lord Beaverbrook, perhaps the greatest of the press barons and a real baron to boot, was asked by Rudyard Kipling what his actual political beliefs were. Kipling was puzzled by the contradictory viewpoints expressed in Beaverbrook's *Daily Express,* which was at that time the best-selling newspaper in the entire world. The answer was revealing. The famous newspaper magnate said bluntly, 'What I want is power. Kiss 'em one day and kick 'em the next.' It was probably having observed Alfred Harmsworth's success in that field which prompted Beaverbrook to speak in this way. He had seen the immense influence which a newspaper proprietor could exert on the affairs of a nation by the example of Harmsworth's *Daily Mail* in the years before the First World War. More particularly, Lord Beaverbrook must have noted the role which the *Daily Mail* played in preparing the British public for that conflict and ensuring that when the time came, men were queuing up and clamouring to be send to the killing fields of France.

It would be going a little too far to suggest that popular newspapers such as the *Daily Mail* were solely responsible for Britain's entry into the Great War, but they certainly played their part in stimulating public support for the war with Germany. Before looking at what the *Daily Mail* was up to, the example of William Randolph Hearst's *New York Journal* may prove instructive.

Hearst acquired the *New York Journal* in 1895 and soon began a fierce campaign to raise circulation and compete with newspapers such as Joseph Pulitzer's *New York World*. A difficulty soon emerged, which was that while splashing on the front page an item about the death of a glamorous actress might boost sales for a day or two, such stories quickly faded. What Hearst wanted was continuing drama that he could publicise day after day, week after week or even month after month. He found a story of this sort in the insurgency raging in Cuba.

Cuba was a Spanish possession in the late nineteenth century. The United States did not view European colonialism favourably, at least not when it was so close to their own country, and so the Americans were vaguely supportive of the rebellion in Cuba against the Spanish authorities there.

William Randolph Hearst was strongly in favour of American intervention in Cuba and he sent one of his employees to the country to cover the crisis there. Frederick Remington was a noted artist, but after spending some time in Cuba, where the fighting had now died down, he wired Hearst, saying 'Everything quiet. There is no trouble here. There will be no war. Wish to return.' Hearst replied, 'Please remain. You furnish the pictures and I'll furnish the war'.

The chance for Hearst to 'furnish the war' came a few months later. In January 1898, the United States sent the battleship *Maine* to Havana to protect American interests. On 15 February, the battleship sank with the loss of 260 sailors, following a tremendous explosion. Although this was probably the result of an accident on board, Hearst's *New York Journal* at once claimed that it had been sunk by a mine planted by Spanish forces. The idea was implausible, but for the next week, the *New York Journal* devoted no fewer than eight pages a day to promoting the notion that Spain was responsible for the disaster. The slogan, 'Remember the *Maine*! To hell with Spain!' featured in this campaign. Public opinion in America was inflamed by the idea that a hostile European power had attacked an American warship and within weeks, the Spanish-American War had begun. Not only was Spain driven from Cuba, but the United States took the opportunity to seize the Philippines too, a Spanish possession on the edge of the South China Sea. The rise of America as a world power dates from the time that the United States began its expansion across the Pacific and laid claim to territories thousands of miles from the North American continent. It was popular journalism which prompted and encouraged this, the first overseas expansionist war in which the United States had ever engaged.

The example of Hearst's political power in encouraging and then exacerbating an international crisis in this way proved attractive to Alfred Harmsworth. The *Daily Mail* was, at the beginning of the twentieth century, already becoming very influential and powerful. We don't have to look very far to see the way in which it was shaping the very way that we see history. One of the most memorable features of the Edwardian years were the women in Britain who were fighting to get the vote. Ask anybody today what these militant campaigners were known as, and you will of course be told that they were suffragettes. The impression is that this was the name they called themselves. In fact, women like the Pankhursts had been known for many years as 'suffragists', those hoping to gain suffrage, or the right to vote in Parliamentary elections. On 10 January 1906, the *Daily Mail* coined the word 'suffragette' to describe the younger and more militant suffragists.

The word was a patronising diminutive. Harmsworth's newspaper, though, had managed to create the term by which the whole struggle for female emancipation has come to be known; even now, over a century later.

Devising a faintly insulting name for women who wanted to have the same rights as their husbands was a relatively harmless exercise on the part of a newspaper. Far more serious was the role played by the *Daily Mail* in stirring up animosity towards Germany and preparing the nation for the slaughter of the First World War. So determined was Lord Northcliffe, as Alfred Harmsworth became in 1905, that Britain would one day find herself fighting Germany, that Alfred Gardiner, editor of the *Daily News*, said after the First World War had begun that, 'Next to the Kaiser, Lord Northcliffe has done more than any other living man to bring about the war.'

William Le Queux was a thriller writer who, in 1906, was commissioned by Northcliffe to provide a novel which was to be serialised in the *Daily Mail*. This was called *The Invasion of 1910* and was a detailed account of how the German army invaded and occupied England. To publicise the story, and stimulate sales of his newspaper, Northcliffe arranged for actors to be hired to dress up as German soldiers and parade up and down Regent Street. Newspaper sellers in the street were also tricked out as German infantry, complete with spiked helmets. Northcliffe took a keen editorial interest in Le Queux's book, insisting that parts of it were changed. He wished to ensure that the most exciting scenes of the fictional Anglo-German war were set in parts of the country where his newspapers were popular. Because of this, the Battle of Royston and the Siege of London became pivotal episodes in the drama.

The *Daily Mail* was full of scare stories about Germans infiltrating Britain, posing as waiters and shopkeepers, while just waiting for the chance to support an invasion when it took place. Boycotts were urged of restaurants employing German staff and the allegation was made that somewhere near London there existed a stockpile of rifles and ammunition ready to be used by these fifth columnists!

In 1906, the year that the *Daily Mail* serialised the story of a German invasion, the newly-elected Liberal government had grand plans for increasing expenditure on the less fortunate in society. There would be old-age pensions, subsidised medical care and a host of other measures, all designed to benefit the ordinary man and woman in the street. It would cost a lot of money, but this could be found through higher taxes for the wealthy and also a reduced defence budget. This was anathema to Lord Northcliffe, who wanted to see more military spending so that Germany could be challenged. In the early spring of 1906 a new type of battleship was launched by Britain. Commissioned by the outgoing Conservative government, HMS *Dreadnought* signalled a radical change in naval warfare. She was so heavily-armed, well-protected and fast that she was, to all intents and purposes, invincible. All other existing battleships were made obsolete once HMS *Dreadnought* went into service.

Building 'Dreadnoughts', as the type became known, was very expensive and the Liberals hoped to be able to focus on domestic expenditure, to tackle the problems of poverty and inequality which had afflicted the country for centuries. They found themselves under pressure from first Northcliffe's *Daily Mail* and then, almost unbelievably, from working-class people themselves to change their priorities and build more warships! Germany had certainly begun building Dreadnoughts of her own and the fear, encouraged by the press, was that Britain and her empire were under threat. So began an arms race which the country could ill afford. This centred around the increasingly strident demands from the British public, urged on by Lord Northcliffe's newspapers, to expand the Royal Navy's capabilities by constructing more Dreadnoughts.

Lord Northcliffe managed to get the socialist Robert Blatchford to write a series of articles for the *Daily Mail* in 1909, which claimed that the British Empire was under threat and that Britain should introduce conscription and go onto a war footing. At a time when the Liberals were trying to force Chancellor Lloyd George's budget through the Lords, in order to make more provision for the elderly, sick and unemployed, Blatchford wrote: 'At the moment the whole country is in a ferment about the budget and the peers and the election. It seems sheer criminal lunacy to waste time and strength chasing such political bubble when the Empire is threatened.' Summing up the desire or need for more Dreadnoughts, George Wyndham MP coined the phrase, 'We want eight and we won't wait!'. Encouraged by the *Daily Mail*, this became a popular chant in music halls. Social welfare could wait, as long as Britain had enough battleships.

The Anglo-German naval arms race culminated, of course, in the outbreak of war between the two countries in the summer of 1914, a war which nobody had done more to promote that Lord Northcliffe and his newspapers. Newspapers had influenced the course of wars before; reports in The *Times* during the Crimean War had even precipitated the fall of a government. Never before though had a British newspaper deliberately set out in this way to cause a conflict. It was only possible because so many people were now reading newspapers and this situation was itself a product of the various technological developments at which we have looked in this chapter.

The awareness of current affairs on the part of the great mass of people in Britain was a relatively new phenomenon, one which the popular press had done much to cultivate and indeed manipulate. Knowledge of what was happening, both in their own country and abroad, was also being brought to people by another of the media which appeared at roughly the same time as cheap newspapers. It is at this new medium, that of the cinema, that we shall next look.

Chapter 4

The Coming of Cinema

The three forms of mass media which emerged at the beginning of the twentieth century all had their roots many years earlier. They had been around for quite a while, but had not flowered before in such profusion. We often read or hear of the ways in which modern electronic technology, the Internet for example or mobile phones, have changed society and altered the way that people behave. Less commonly are we invited to consider the opposite case; how people's behaviour has shaped the technology. It is easy to forget that this is a two-way street. If the existence of the World Wide Web has had a great effect upon us, we have been equally influential in creating the Web and deciding what it should be like. The same goes for mobile phones. They have certainly given rise to a new code of etiquette and brought about a change, some would say a decline, in manners, but smartphones are themselves a product of our needs and desires.

Just as with the information technology of the early twenty-first century, so too with the development of new media in the opening years of the twentieth century. Take cinema. When films were first shown in this country, they were typically projected in music halls, at the end of the main show, or in tents set up at travelling fairs. Almost invariably, these short films were documentaries or newsreels, although they weren't known by those names at the time. The short clips of real-life events which covered some newsworthy incident were called 'topicals'. Companies like Biograph sent cameramen out into the world to film real-life people, places and events for the edification of music-hall audiences. Their advertising slogan was 'The Biograph reproduces the latest events from all parts of the world'. Cinema was thus seen initially as something informative and educational, a way of showing the working-class patrons of the music halls scenes of the world about them. The first public display of projected films took place in France in 1895 and the titles of some of the short films in the programme tell us all that we need know about early cinema! We have such riveting features as *The Demolition of a Wall* and *Workers Leaving the Lumière Factory*. Other films at that time showed circus performers or animals and sometimes celebrities, the kind of people that nobody in the audience at the average music hall was likely to catch sight of in real life. They were thus a little like today's television news.

In a previous chapter, we saw how demand determined the nature and use of inventions such as the stereoscope and phonograph. Thomas Edison, inventor of the phonograph, had it in mind that his creation would primarily be used for educational purposes, but today we know that 99 per cent of the records produced for phonographs and gramophones were designed purely and solely for entertainment. This demand fashioned the companies which were producing records and dictated the course of their business activities. So too did the Edwardians ensure that cinema abandoned all efforts to inform and educate the audiences and focused instead only upon entertaining them.

For an account of the typical reaction to these travelogues and newsreels from working-class men and women who had come to see a variety show, we cannot do better than turn once more to J.B. Priestley, who was a young man in the Edwardian period. He wrote of visiting the music hall with friends:

> The final act in most of these variety shows when all the glory of the programme had vanished, was a few minutes of jerky film, generally called 'Bioscope'. But we rarely stayed to discover what the Bioscope was offering us. Now that we have so many accounts of the early history of films, we know that men in various places were taking them very seriously indeed. But that was true of very few people. My friends and I waved them away.

If this was the attitude of a middle-class youth to being educated and informed in this way, one can only imagine how the crowds of ordinary working men and women reacted. It was the reaction of these first, overwhelmingly working-class, viewers which was largely responsible for the cinema's evolution into an art form devoted purely to entertainment; that is to say the direction cinema took was shaped by the reception of these early non-fiction films. If the new medium *did* have any effect upon the audience, then it is equally true that the audience greatly affected the medium itself.

We have seen that Edwardian Britain was very similar to our own time, with many of the same worries and concerns that people in the country still have. Violent crime, terrorism, uncontrolled immigration, Eastern Europeans supposedly taking jobs from native-born Britons, riots, industrial action, international crises; all these were regular features of life in Britain between the death of Queen Victoria and the beginning of the First World

War. There were even fears about the ill-effects which new media might be having upon children. We are all of us familiar with claims that children don't read as much as they used to, because they are spending so long on their mobiles and tablets. In Nottingham, in 1913, the claim was being made that the borrowing of books from children's libraries in the city had dropped by 50 per cent. The reason? Children were now spending all their leisure time at cinemas and could no longer be bothered to read!

There was nothing new about the *concept* of cinema. Audiences were being diverted and amused by seeing moving images being projected on screens at least two centuries before the arrival of films. Magic lanterns, crude projectors which allowed pictures painted on glass slides to be shown, greatly enlarged, on blank walls, were written about and described in the seventeenth century. By 1710, a company called Reeves of London was producing magic lantern slides which showed moving objects, for example a cockroach jumping into the mouth of a sleeping man. Such effects, which brought scenes to life, became very popular in the eighteenth and nineteenth centuries. Windmills with turning sails, ships tossing on a stormy sea, animals jumping over a fence – all relied on one glass slide being moved relative to another; which remained stationery.

There was of course a limit to how effective such things could be in reproducing realistic scenes and they were sometimes combined with the so-called 'dissolving view', where two or three magic lanterns were combined, allowing one scene to fade or dissolve into another. In this way, a vista of green fields in the summer could gradually be transformed into a snowy landscape. As with moving slides though, the range of what could be presented in this way was still narrow.

The magic lantern was one precursor of the cinema. Another was the Victorian parlour toy known variously as the Phenakistoscope or Fantascope. This was a revolving, slotted disc which was viewed in front of a mirror. A series of coloured drawings, each slightly different from the other, merged into an illusion of continuous movement, due to the physiological process known as 'persistence of vision'. Any image seen by our eyes is retained for a tenth of a second or so. If the first image is rapidly replaced by a second and then a third; our mind merges them together and the impression we have is one of continuity and flowing motion. It is upon this optical illusion that cinema still relies.

Of course, schoolboys have known for centuries about this phenomenon. Drawings made on the corners of a book could be brought to life if the pages were flicked through quickly enough. This sort of thing was a common amusement of children throughout the nineteenth century. The novel *Vice Versa*, first published in 1882, describes a father investigating the contents of his son's pockets. He finds, among other things, '. . . a broken prism from a crystal chandelier, a gilded Jew's harp, a little book in which the leaves on being turned briskly, gave a semblance of motion to the sails of a black windmill drawn therein . . .'. Flip books based on this principle were marketed in Britain from the 1860s onwards; at first with drawn figures and animals, but later consisting of a series of posed photographs. These developed into the one of the earliest methods ways of viewing moving pictures; the mechanical device patented in America in 1894, as the Mutoscope.

The Mutoscope was essentially a flip book of photographs secured into a frame within a peep-show type of machine. Only one person at a time could view the pictures, which were photographs printed onto stout, flexible card and secured firmly at one end. When a coin had been placed in the slot, an electric lamp came on to illuminate the pictures and by turning a crank handle, they would be flipped through and the illusion of motion created. Many of these arcade machines had a slightly risqué theme, which led to their being known in Britain as 'What the butler saw' machines. A typical Mutoscope held about 850 photographs, which made for a minute or so of viewing. At fourteen frames a second, this was a flickering and jerky experience, but these machines were tremendously popular. Although early Mutoscope features included such innocuous topics as a man walking a tightrope, it was soon apparent where the real market lay. We have already seen this trend when we looked at phonographs and stereoscopes in an earlier chapter. To begin with, the aim is laudable, typically intending to be informative and educational, but soon they turn to what is most profitable; in this case, pornography. By the time that Queen Victoria died, it was widely recognized on both sides of the Atlantic, that the commonest use of the Mutoscope was for viewing images of half-, or even completely, naked women.

By the time of the Edwardians, the Mutoscope's sleazy image was an acknowledged fact of life. At first, they had been installed in all sorts of public places, but this had caused problems, as women and children were innocently putting their pennies in the slot and duly having their sensibilities outraged. In the late 1890s, railway companies installed them on station platforms as a means of generating revenue, although this practice ended when the implications became apparent. At Rhyl station in north Wales, a Mutoscope was placed openly on the platform, until complaints about the unsuitability of the mildly suggestive scenes depicted, led to its being relocated in the men's lavatories. This did not end the controversy, because it was alleged that the railway company were profiting from vice by charging people to view such dreadful images.

The fuss about Rhyl railway station's 'What the butler saw' machine even reached the pages of the *Times*. A letter sent to the paper in 1899 talked of, 'the corruption of the young which comes from exhibiting under a strong light, nude female figures represented as living and moving, going in and out of baths . . .'. The machine at Rhyl was removed soon afterwards.

Throughout the Edwardian years, penny-in-the-slot machines of the type described above became a standard feature of seaside amusement arcades. Whatever those who wrote angry letters to the *Times* might say, they were in general seen as a bit of harmless, saucy fun; a little like the seaside postcards of Donald McGill. Those who put their pennies in the slot knew very well by that time what they were likely to see and the prudes simply avoided them.

In Chapter 10, we shall be considering the durability of the technology used by the Edwardians and the Mutoscope provides us with an excellent example of this. The cast-iron frames of those old penny-in-the-slot machines were virtually indestructible. The internal mechanism too was extremely simply and robust. All that could really go wrong was that the light bulb needed to be changed from time to time. Because of this, Mutoscopes lingered on in British amusement arcades until the 1970s. It was the introduction of decimal currency in 1971 which delivered the *coup de grâce* to these quaint antiques. It was found to be very difficult and expensive to convert them to accept the new coinage and so most were simply sold off for scrap metal. One or two examples have found their way to museums and these are still working as well today as they were before the First World War. It is interesting to speculate whether any of today's gadgets are likely to be similarly long-lived!

Another type of peepshow featuring moving images was Thomas Edison's Kinetoscope. This, like the Mutoscope, did not project moving pictures onto a screen and so cannot really be classified as cinema. Instead, a continuous loop of standard film was viewed through a magnifying lens. One could gaze at brief clips of moving pictures very much like the 'What the butler saw' machine, although usually without the semi-pornographic association of the Mutoscope. Edison's machines were set up in amusement arcades and for a small sum, one could see Buffalo Bill, Annie Oakley or various circus acts or comic sketches. The Kinetoscope very slightly predated the Mutoscope, being first presented to the public in May 1893.

The first Kinetoscope parlour opened in New York a year later. It contained ten Kinetoscopes and for 50c, one could view all of them. For 25c, it was possible to see just five of the machines. The films, contained on endless loops, were as short as those in the Mutoscope; although somewhat less interesting! A blacksmith at work shoeing horses, a trapeze artiste and a wrestler were some of the clips of film on offer. These early films were what came to be known as 'actuality' films and they were the forerunner of documentaries. For over ten years, this was to be the chief fare in moving pictures; brief clips showing people doing various things. There was no narrative, these films were far too short for that. Sometimes, there would be brief scenes of slapstick humour, but in the main, ordinary life was simply presented as it appeared to the camera.

The Kinetoscope craze did not last long. At one point, Thomas Edison tried to liven his films up a little by adding sound from a phonograph, but really these little films were nothing more than a novelty. The American film expert Tom Gunn coined the expression 'cinema of attractions' to describe what films were like in the years up until 1906 or 1907. We are so used to watching cinema actors in the modern world, who are seemingly oblivious of the cameras which are recording their actions, that we hardly notice any more the conventions to which they abide. The first films shown to the paying public were very different. Many of them were panoramic views of the natural world or city streetscapes. In those which did feature actors, they tended to play for the camera, as though they were on the stage in a music hall and trying to make eye contact with the viewer. In short, the selling point of early cinema was not that anything much was happening; it was the novelty of simply seeing moving photographs. This was the attraction in itself.

It is easy to laugh at the naiveté of those who would be entranced by a minute or so of film showing something as trivial as a performing animal or perhaps a man shaving. One of the earliest bits of film we have comes from Edison's studio in 1894 and shows a man called Fred Ott taking a pinch of snuff and sneezing. It lasts just five seconds. When we think a little more about this sort of thing though, we become uncomfortably aware that these same kinds of film-clips are immensely popular, even in the twenty-first century! A direct line may be drawn from the short 'actuality' films featured in the Kinetoscope parlours to the modern-day cult of YouTube.

Cinema is essentially a social activity. We sit among crowds of people, most of them strangers but perhaps a few of them our friends, and watch a public display rather like an old-time magic lantern show. The Mutoscope and Kinetoscope were, by contrast, private pleasures, in which only one person at a time viewed and was entertained by the moving images. Today, the private viewing of clips of films showing cute animals, human mishaps or remarkable real-life scenes is a big part of many young people's lives. Some of them spend hours on YouTube, gazing endlessly at exactly the same kind of brief 'actuality' films which so entranced their great-great-grandparents. This is no shared activity like going to the cinema; these people are watching a cabinet of curiosities, a peepshow of odd and remarkable things from the real world. It is important to note the difference between this sort of thing and the social activity of going to the cinema, which in the Edwardian period became such a popular pastime among working-class people. Of course, before cinema could arrive, a method had to be found to project films onto walls and screens.

Some time in the 1870s – the exact date is hotly debated – an Englishman called Eadweard Muybridge experimented in the United States by taking twelve photographs of a galloping horse in quick succession. The aim was to settle a bet about whether all four of a horse's hoofs are off the ground simultaneously when galloping; the eventual result was the first projected, photographic moving images. Muybridge devised a way to project the photographs one after the other onto a screen and called this machine the Zoogyroscope. The magazine *Scientific American* reported a meeting of the San Francisco Art Association on 4 May 1880, at which Eadweard Muybridge showed one of his projections on a screen which depicted, according to the author of the piece in *Scientific American,* '. . . apparently the living, moving animals. Nothing was wanting but the clatter of hoofs upon the turf.' This was a repeating image, like those shown in the parlour toy known as the Fantascope, just twelve photographs shown again and again in quick succession.

Once cellulose nitrate became widely available, then long strips of film could be used to extend the running time of the entertainment. Even a single minute of cinema requires almost a hundred feet of film and a full-length feature film needs somewhere in the region of a mile and a half. Not that any of the films being shown at the time at which we are looking were anything remotely as long as the films we have today. There would have been little point really, because they were not narratives at all, as we understand cinema films now to be.

There was some opposition to the idea of films being projected and becoming an entertainment for a large audience. Thomas Edison, for one, thought it a terrible idea to project films for a large audience, rather than keeping them as the strictly personal experience of peering through a peephole into a Kinetoscope. When people were growing excited about projectors, he said:

> If we make this screen machine that you are asking for, it will spoil everything. We are making these peep show machines and selling a lot of them at a good profit. If we put out a screen machine there will be a use for about ten of them in the whole United States. With that many screen machines you could show the pictures to everybody in the country – and then it would be done. Let's not kill the goose that lays the golden egg.

Which only goes to show how even the most far-sighted and visionary of men can at times be unbelievably blinkered and wrongheaded in their estimations of what the future holds!

The first films screened for an audience in Britain were shown at the headquarters of the Royal Photographic Society in London's Hanover Square on 14 January 1896. The films included *The Opening of the Kiel Canal, Rough Seas at Dover* and *The Derby*. These were fairly typical of what was being offered for the next few years. There was no attempt at any sort of narrative to begin with, which is why topical events were a popular subject. Sometimes, comic sequences were filmed, of the kind which would be seen in a music hall, but the whole aim was simply to demonstrate the technical abilities of the new medium.

There has lately been much debate in Britain about the phenomenon of 'fake news', that is to say spurious items of news which crop up on the Internet and are believed by many people to be true. We are also familiar with skilfully-altered photographs which appear very convincing at first sight. This sort of deception was a feature of early newsreel films and such impostures were accepted uncritically by audiences because it never occurred to anybody that a film of some battle would be anything other than a plain and unadorned record of what had taken place. There was in fact an entire industry in the early years of cinema which was devoted to deceiving audiences and persuading them that they were watching actual events. Some of these frauds from the late nineteenth and early twentieth centuries might be regarded as the earliest acted narratives!

During the Russo-Japanese War of 1904–5, there was huge demand for up-to-date film from the front, which companies in Europe were happy to provide. They did this by engaging crowds of people and kitting them out in generic army uniforms and then filming them charging towards some distant objective. Hey presto: the storming of Port Arthur in China! People were not used to seeing moving films in those days, which meant that if what were purported to be battleships were shown, partly obscured by clouds of smoke, it was easy to persuade viewers that these really were Japanese warships bombarding the Russian fleet. In fact, the ships were toys and the smoke provided by fireworks.

A slightly later example of this kind of thing will show why these tricks qualify as 'fake news' and were horribly misleading. There is, even to this day, a myth that during the Russian Revolution of October 1917, the Winter Palace in St Petersburg was 'stormed'. Indeed, the 'storming' of the Winter Palace is one of the most well-known episodes of the revolution. Illustration 9 shows the storming of the Winter Palace. It is an image with which many readers are likely to be familiar. This one may be found in a well-regarded history of the events of 1917, *The Russian Revolution* by Alan Moorehead.

The truth is that there was no 'storming' of the Winter Palace at all. By the time that the Bolsheviks had seized all the other public buildings in St Petersburg, then known as Petrograd, the defenders of the Winter Palace had nearly all deserted. It was entered peacefully through an unlocked side door, without a single shot being fired. A few years later, the Soviet government staged a 're-enactment' of the event, showing troops, supported by an armoured car, fighting their way into the heavily-defended palace. A film was also made of the event and it is stills from this which are still being passed off as photographs of the actual event. Fake news is not a modern phenomenon.

The opening years of film-shows in Britain fixed forever the way in which they would be regarded culturally, right down to the present day. To begin with, film projectors would be set up in a tent as part of a travelling entertainment, a little like a carnival sideshow. Indeed, a lot of such exhibitions travelled with fairs and circuses. Later, the films would be shown at the end of a music-hall programme. Both fairs and music halls were almost exclusively working-class environments and the pattern set then lasted for the whole of the Edwardian period, even when purpose-built cinemas began to be built. Cinema and films were inextricably linked to the lower classes and although middle and upper-class people might visit the new cinemas from time to time, there was a definite feeling that this was not something which was expected of their class. They were, quite consciously, 'slumming it'. Such sentiments linger on to this day. We are all of us subconsciously aware that opera, ballet and the theatre belong in the sphere of high culture in a way that cinema films do not! This instinctive feeling is a relic from the early days of cinema in Britain.

From being little more than a cultural footnote, cinema grew rapidly from 1900 to 1912, until it was a major influence on working-class life in Britain. The first purpose-built cinema in the country opened at Colne in Lancashire on 22 February 1907. It was the brainchild of Joshua Duckworth, who had previously been a magic lantern showman. Just five years later, there were estimated to be over 4,000 cinemas in Britain; a figure which was to remain largely unchanged until the Second World War. During the years between 1907 and 1912, cinemas sprang up in almost unbelievable profusion. Nine were opened in one London suburb alone and Glasgow had no fewer than eighty-five. By 1914, over eight million tickets were being sold each week. Going to 'the pictures' had become by far and away the most popular pastime of working-class people.

Of course, things were very different when the film show was situated in one fixed place, rather than travelling around the country. If your audience is constantly changing, then you can show the same thing over and over again, first in one town and then the next. When the same people will be coming next week as were at your show this week then obviously a different programme is required, one which changes from week to week. At the time, even fiction films or photoplays as they were sometimes known, lasted only ten minutes, twenty or thirty at most. The ninety-minute feature films with which we are so familiar had not yet been thought of. This meant that the programme in those Edwardian cinemas was a lot more varied than that which we now see.

These days when we go to the cinema, we expect to see one long film, with various advertisements thrown in as well. Well within living memory, up until the 1960s, the typical programme at the cinema was very different. At that time, there would be two films; the main feature and a second film, which was known as the B film. In addition to this, there would cartoons and a newsreel. Until 1970, the Pathé newsreel was a fixed point in a visit to the cinema, although by that time most people were seeing the latest news on their televisions, rather than relying upon Pathé. Another throwback to the earlier era of Edwardian cinema-going was the custom of coming in late to a film and then watching the end and staying to see the part of the film which was missed. This practice gave rise to the expression, 'This is where we came in!'

Before the First World War, cinema performances tended to be medleys of short clips, few longer than ten or fifteen minutes. For example, the first

Western, and incidentally the first blockbuster ever made, was *The Great Train Robbery*. This film, which was made in America but was enormously successful also in Britain, set the trend for films which were fictional narratives, rather than merely curiosities. It was very different from, say, the fifteen-minute-long *Lady Contortionist*, made four years before, which was simply a circus performer going through her repertoire. *The Great Train Robbery* was atypical of the content of most cinema programmes before feature films came to the fore, but it was a harbinger of the future

What is surprising about Edwardian cinema is that it rapidly became very sophisticated in various ways. In fact, a lot of the developments which we think of as not taking place until much later in the century, were actually first seen before the First World War. Talkies, which most of us associate with the 1920s, made their appearance twenty years earlier.

It's the one thing that everybody knows about cinema; that *The Jazz Singer*, starring Al Jolson, was the first 'talkie'. This was the film, released in 1927, which marked the beginning of the end for the silent movies which was all that anybody had known up to that time. Al Jolson's line, 'Wait a minute, you ain't heard nothin' yet', has become iconic as ushering in the modern world of cinema (although for some strange reason, it is almost invariably misremembered as, 'You ain't heard nothin' yet *folks!*'). What nobody ever seems to remember is that *The Jazz Singer* contained, in addition to its songs, just two minutes of spoken dialogue. All the rest was flashed onto the screen in the form of printed titles, just as in any silent film. The method used for both the music and dialogue was one which had been in use for well over twenty years. It was a system of gramophone records synchronized mechanically with the projector. There was in fact nothing in the least bit novel about *The Jazz Singer*, other than the fact that it was the first full-length feature film to use this primitive method.

The first films with sound were produced by Thomas Edison as early as 1894. That was the year that a seventeen-second clip of film was made, showing a man playing a violin and two other men dancing. The film shows that the violinist is playing in front of an enormous horn, which looks as though it must be at least six feet long. This is a clue to what was happening, because this is a recording horn for one of Edison's phonograph machines; which recorded sound on wax cylinders. The film had been known for many years and the cylinder associated with it turned up in the 1960s. It was not until 1998 that the two were combined though and the result is the world's first film with an accompanying soundtrack.

Edison's crude method was developed commercially into the Kinetophone, which linked one of his Kinetoscopes to a phonograph and was then marketed as a complete unit. There was no attempt to synchronize the film with the cylinder and only a small number of Kinetophones were eventually produced. The idea itself though, of films linked to phonograph or gramophone records, was to shape the development of cinema for many years, both in Britain and the United States.

The first synchronized sound films, actual talking pictures, were shown at the Paris Exposition on 8 June 1900. Produced by the Gaumont company, the films were extracts from five plays, including *Hamlet*. Among the artistes featured was Sarah Bernhardt. That same year, the Bio-Tableaux Films company was screening similar films in Britain. Music-hall performers such as Vesta Tilley sang on film twenty-seven years before Al Jolson, using a precisely similar method of gramophone records coordinated with cinema projectors.

There were two great problems to be solved with exploiting talking movies during the Edwardian years. The first of these was that none of the systems being developed was automatic. All relied to a greater or less extent upon the projectionist working frantically to ensure that the sound and picture were precisely aligned. This was no easy task. The Cinephone method, which first appeared in 1908, is a case in point. The projectionist was obliged, in addition to changing the reels and adjusting the focus, to keep his eye on a little clock face on the screen, while at the same time watching an illuminated pointer elsewhere on screen. While doing this, he had to wind a handle which kept the clock face and pointer in the same position. Inevitably, errors were made. A momentary lapse in attention and the soundtrack was soon out of synchronization with the film.

The Vivaphone was another early way of playing gramophone records simultaneously with projected films. This was a little simpler, in that only one icon, a pointer, had to be constantly adjusted until it was vertical. Vivaphone made films of a number of British politicians from 1910 onwards. These included Bonar Law, who later became Prime Minister, and Lord Birkenhead. It was even agreed that the Vivaphone company, run by Cecil Hepworth, could make a 'talkie' of a Cabinet meeting held at 10 Downing Street; although ultimately nothing came of this.

Oddly enough, despite eventually losing interest in the idea of talking pictures, it was Thomas Edison who came up with the idea which eventually made possible the production of films such as *The Jazz Singer*. After a lot of initial reluctance, Edison became a convert to the projection of films from his Kinetoscope. He redesigned the Kinetoscope so that it could be used to project films onto a screen and marketed it as the world's first home cinema. The projecting Kinetoscope was not a commercial success – the public were not yet ready for the idea of watching movies in the comfort of their own homes – but it led to an improvement in adding sound to films.

In 1913, Edison unveiled the latest version of the projecting Kinetoscope, which was intended to be the last word in talking pictures. The by-now hopelessly outdated cylinder phonograph was linked to the projector by a series of pulleys and belts, which made the synchronization of film with soundtrack more reliable than any of the other methods then being used. It was a flop, however, partly because the reproduction of sound on the cylinders was atrocious, but also because there was no reliable way of amplifying the sound. Besides, the whole idea of recording film and sound separately and then trying to coordinate their playback was a blind alley. The future lay with having the soundtrack being an integral part of the film, although this was not obvious to everybody at that time. Which was of course why the 'first talkie' in 1927 still relied upon a Heath-Robinson arrangement of mechanical connections to make sure that the gramophone records were playing at the right part of the film. The first sound-on-film system was invented in London as early as 1907, although it was not a commercial success. Eugene Laust, who had at one time worked with Thomas Edison, devised a most ingenious way of imprinting a soundtrack next to the images on a standard 35mm film. The difficulties of producing cinema films with accompanying sound were solved by one person. This was Lee de Forest, about whom a great deal will be said in Chapter 8. For now, it is enough to observe that it was de Forest who invented the world's first electronic amplifier in 1906. This was the triode; the Audion vacuum tube, which boosted current and was the basis for electronics for the next half century. In 1912, Lee de Forest experimented with an early magnetic recording machine and managed to amplify the sound from it. This was vital if cinema and radio were to become mass media and public entertainments. The sound from Thomas Edison's Kinetophone was so faint that it had to be listened to through twin tubes, resembling a stethoscope. Only electronic amplifiers could solve this difficulty.

Most people, if asked, would guess that colour films began appearing not long before the Second World War. That's certainly when the first colour films of which most of us are aware were made. Our minds turn to *Gone With the Wind* and *The Wizard of Oz*, both released in 1939, and Errol Flynn in *The Adventures of Robin Hood* the year before. Films from the 1920s were all in black-and-white, weren't they? And we know that all the film of the First World War was in black-and-white. It is odd therefore to consider that cinema films in colour were quite a big thing as early as 1908 and that they played a large role in persuading middle-class people that the cinema was not just some vulgar pursuit which their servants undertook on their evenings off.

The very first colour films were made just before the end of the nineteenth century, but there was little chance of their ever being exploited commercially. The reason for this is that it while proved simple enough to make the films, it proved quite impossible to devise a projector capable of showing them!

Producing natural colours in photographs is a complicated process; it is far more difficult than ordinary black-and-white photography. For this reason, the first colour photography used black-and-white images, cleverly manipulated. The same method was used in the earliest colour films; that is to say black-and-white film was used. On 17 May 1861, the physicist James Clerk Maxwell demonstrated some results of his research on colour vision. Maxwell was perhaps the greatest scientist of the nineteenth century, the man who came up with a theory which unified magnetism and electricity and showed them both to be aspects of a single force, and when he gave his lecture at the Royal Institution in London, the audience were prepared to be surprised. They were not disappointed. The scientist had photographed a tartan ribbon three times in black-and-white, each time placing a different filter over the camera lens. These were red, green and blue. In the darkened lecture theatre, Maxwell used three magic lanterns to project the photographs which he taken of the ribbon. Each picture was projected through a lens of the same colour as that used as a filter when the image was originally captured. The effect was stunning; the tartan ribbon was shown on the screen in its original colours. Nothing like this had ever been seen before and the hall erupted in applause.

There was, of course, one slight disadvantage of the method which the famous scientist had come up with for taking colour pictures: it was quite impossible to print pictures in this way. It was to be eighty years before anybody was able to produce a permanent coloured print of the ribbon from those black-and-white negatives. Nevertheless, by the end of the nineteenth century there were those who glimpsed a way of exploiting this strange system to solve another problem; that of showing colour films on a cinema screen.

On 22 March 1899, Edward Turner and Frederick Lee applied for a patent in Britain for the world's first method of making moving pictures in colour. This did not use colour film, like the later Technicolor system. Instead, an ingenious mechanical camera and corresponding projector were used. Three successive frames were filmed through red, green and blue filters. By projecting the resulting film through those same three coloured filters, they would be combined and the illusion of natural colour created. It would be as effective as Maxwell's spectacular demonstration forty years earlier. That at least was the theory. In practice, it was easy enough to make the films but showing them on a screen was so beset with difficulties that it ultimately proved impossible. For one thing, any moving object would be in different positions in each of the frames, which would mean that the red, blue and green versions of the shots would not be synchronized. Not only that, but trying to superimpose even still shots, one perfectly upon the other, was beyond the technology of the time. Everything appeared on the screen surrounded by prismatic hazes, which wavered and flickered distractingly.

After making films with the newly-invented process in 1901 and 1902, it became plain that Turner's method was a flop and no attempt was made to market it. He died in 1903 and the films which he had made ended up ultimately in a storeroom at the Science Museum in London, where they lay forgotten for many years. In 2012, they found their way to Bradford's National Media Museum, where they were digitally restored. It was found that with modern editing equipment, superimposing the separate images one upon the other was a fairly straightforward, if laborious, task. In 2012, the results were shown in public and they created a minor sensation. The colours of Turner's pet parrot and his children playing with flowers were as vivid and sharp as anything filmed decades later using Technicolor. The world's first colour films, using a process patented during the reign of Queen Victoria, were now seen to have been stunningly successful.

The first commercially-successful process for making cinema films in natural colour was that invented by George Albert Smith of Brighton in 1906. It was in many ways like Turner's system. The camera, which ran at twice the speed of ordinary cinema cameras at that time, shot ordinary black-and-white film on alternate frames; one through a red filter and the next through a green one. The filters rotated rapidly on an aluminium wheel, so that first one and then the other was behind the camera lens. When showing the completed film, the projector simply replicated this process, with one frame through the red filter and the next through the green. Surprisingly, this bizarre arrangement yielded astonishingly lifelike effects. By reducing the colour filters from three, as in Turner's earlier system, to just two, it became possible to project the images without too much blurring, although faint coloured haloes were still visible at times.

The first public presentation of films shot in Kinemacolour, which is what George Smith called his system, was at the Palace Theatre in Shaftsbury Avenue on 26 February 1909. The programme consisted of twenty-one very short films. These ranged from the Band of the Queen's Highlanders marching along the front at Brighton to yachts at Southwick. The following month, the Natural Colour Kinematograph Co. was established and George Smith went into partnership with Charles Urban.

The first colour film that the new company released was called *A Visit to the Seaside* and was in the nature of a newsreel, showing different aspects of Brighton at the height of summer. It had been filmed in 1908. Bathing machines, children eating ice cream, a panorama across the beach, all in glorious colour. It looked as though colour films were the future of cinema and yet they didn't last. By 1914, colour films had yet to become anywhere near as popular as those in black-and-white. There were several reasons for this. Showing Kinemacolour films required cinemas to invest in the special projector required; which was expensive. It also meant reducing the size of the screen and so limiting the number of customers to the venue. This was because the projected light was not as strong as in black-and-white films, because it had to pass through filters. To compensate for this, the area upon which the film was projected had to be considerably smaller than that used in showing an ordinary black-and-white film. Nor was this the only difficulty. Because of the filters used when filming, films could only be produced in very strong sunlight, not always that common in Britain. As a result, the Natural Colour Kinematograph Co was unable to supply the 300 cinemas and halls which had installed Kinemacolour equipment with regular new films. This meant that the venues were losing customers, as people expected a change of programme at least once a week. Despite these shortcomings, and the fact that colour films did not really take off for another thirty years, Kinemacolour revolutionized the way that cinema was regarded in Britain and transformed it from a vulgar, working-class entertainment into a leisure activity suitable for middle or even upper-class patrons. This was achieved as a result of the most ambitious film ever made using Kinemacolour.

As we have seen, visiting the cinema was, for at least the first ten or twelve years of the twentieth century, seen as an exclusively working-class pleasure. The showing of films began in Britain in music halls and fairgrounds and even when they were being shown in purpose-built cinemas, the feeling persisted that this was not really the thing for anybody who was educated. It was the Natural Colour Kinematograph Co. which changed this perception and made cinema-going an acceptable pastime for all strata of society. The catalyst for this change was an epic, two-and-a-half-hour long documentary made in December 1911 and January 1912. It was called *With Our King and Queen Through India* and it covered the Delhi Durbar which took place after George V's coronation. The King and Queen had travelled to India after the coronation, so that the new King could officially be declared Emperor of India.

Although a total of two-and-a-half hours of film was brought back from India, not all cinemas showed the whole thing. There were twenty-two sections in all and a selection was generally shown at each screening. The exception was at the premiere on 2 February 1912, which took place at the Scala Theatre in London. This was an exceptionally grand affair, with a full orchestra, special lighting effects and a live spoken commentary.

On 11 May 1912, King George V visited the Scala to see *With Our King and Queen Through India*. He was accompanied by his wife, Queen Mary, and his mother, Queen Alexandra. With them was Maria Feodnorovna, Dowager Empress of Russia. The royal party greatly enjoyed the film and were astonished at the colourful spectacle. They liked it so much that later that year, on 12 December, the King arranged for the film to be shown again; this time at Buckingham Palace. After her visit to the Scala Theatre, the Empress Maria wrote to her son, Tsar Nicholas II. She said in her letter: 'We are lunching today with Georgie and May at Buckingham Palace. They both send you greetings. Last night we saw their journey to India. Kinemacolour is wonderfully interesting and very beautiful and gives one the impression of having seen it all in reality.' There is no doubt that this colour film of their state visit was a hit with the royal family, being in effect like a home movie for them of an exciting episode in their lives.

The news that the King and Queen had been to the cinema was electrifying for the snobs who had previously shunned this as a low form of entertainment. It had, after all, now been given the royal seal of approval. Middle-class men and women flocked to see *With Our King and Queen Through India*. It was the fashionable thing to do now and those who had not yet seen this wonderful film began to feel left out. It was this production which began the slow swing to acceptance of cinema among the wider population. As a first introduction to the medium, the film of the Delhi Durbar could hardly bettered.

Other companies were also making films in colour at this time. In the same year that *With Our King and Queen Through India* was released, a three-colour process was demonstrated in France. On 15 November 1912, the new Gaumont Chronochrome colour film was screened to an audience of members of the French Photographic Society in Paris. Instead of the two filters used in Kinemacolour, Chronochrome used three lenses, each covered by a filter of one of the three primary colours. These were all recombined when the films were being projected; which was a fantastically complicated process which nobody had yet managed. It will be recalled that Edward Turner's earlier attempt at this method had been a failure. This first display was designed to showcase the possibilities of Chronochrome and the subjects were chosen for their varied colours; butterflies, gardens and a selection of rural scenes.

On 16 January 1913, Chronochrome reached London and was well received. In some ways, it was superior to Kinemacolour. The range of shades was much greater and the irritating luminous halos which were sometimes visible around subjects filmed in Kinemacolour were wholly absent. In June, a landmark was reached when a series of humorous sketches filmed in Chronochrome were shown at the 39th Street Theatre in New York. These were accompanied by a synchronized soundtrack from a phonograph. Twenty-four years before *The Jazz Singer* and a year before the start of the First World War, colour talkies were being screened! The story of Edwardian colour films continued in 1914, when on 9 April the world's first full-length feature film in natural colour was released. Called *The World, the Flesh and the Devil*, it was an hour and forty minutes long.

By the time that war broke out in the summer of 1914, all the major developments in cinema, which would be endlessly refined over the rest of the century, had already been made. Talkies, films in natural colour, newsreels, full-length feature films, soundtracks on film; all were invented or greatly improved upon during the opening years of the century. For some reason though, we have been afflicted with a kind of selective amnesia, which prevents us from knowing about colour films being made before the First World War and causes us to view *The Jazz Singer*, with its meagre 354 words of dialogue, as the first 'talkie'.

Cinema was the most popular pastime of working-class people throughout much of the twentieth century, until it was eclipsed by television in the 1950s and 1960s. Together with the popular newspapers, which appeared in Britain at roughly the same time as films began to be shown, cinema acted to make people more informed about current affairs; to draw them into political life and involve them in the affairs of the nation. Seeing the Pathé newsreels of Emily Davison hurling herself under the King's horse at

Epsom or watching the army fight a gun battle with foreign terrorists forced people to ask themselves questions about what was going on in their country. Even fifty years earlier, the average person would most probably not have heard about such events; now, they were able to see them taking place before their very eyes.

Cinema-going had become an established habit in Britain before the First World War. The third of the media at which we shall be looking, radio, was only just getting going at that time. Nevertheless, so important was the radio to become for everybody, it is worth examining its roots, which also lie in the Edwardian period. This will form the subject of the next chapter.

Chapter 5

How 'Wireless' Began

Newspapers and cinema were both around before the death of Queen Victoria; in the case of newspapers, their appearance predated her ascent to the throne by 200 years. Radio, on the other hand, was an exciting novelty, whose potential was quite unknown. In that respect, the Edwardian view of radio was analogous to the situation with the Internet in the early 1990s. Nobody had the faintest idea what, if anything, this new phenomenon would mean for ordinary people.

One of the earliest demonstrations of communication by radio waves took place in London in 1879. The existence of invisible electromagnetic waves had been predicted some years earlier by the physicist James Clerk Maxwell, although nobody had yet managed to provide evidence for this new form of energy. Professor David Edward Hughes was born in London in 1831, although his family later moved to the United States. He became a professor of music and while still living in America in 1855, patented the first printing telegraph, designed to give a permanent record of telegraph messages. Two years later, he moved back to London and it was there, in 1877, that he invented the loose-contact carbon microphone, which was to be the standard microphone for the next hundred years. He refused to patent this invention, because he thought that it was too important and should be freely available to the world. There are similarities here to Sir Tim Berners-Lee's decision not to patent his work on the World Wide Web, but rather present it freely as a gift, for the benefit of humanity.

In 1879, Hughes was living at 40 Langham Street, only a minute's walk from where the BBC's Broadcasting House now stands. He was experimenting with a microphone and found that an electric spark produced a discernible and distinctive sound in a telephone earpiece which was not connected to it by any wires. After establishing that this effect was observable in any room in his house, Hughes decided to expand the area of his experiments. He arranged for a clockwork motor periodically to break a circuit and so produce a spark and then set off along Great Portland Street with his receiver. To his amazement, he found that the signals increased in strength until he was sixty yards from his home, following which they began to fade. He was still able to detect them over a quarter of a mile from his circuit-breaker apparatus.

This was an extraordinary discovery and after testing his equipment and double-checking his results for error, he invited two prominent scientists to witness the effect. Sir W.H. Preece and Sir William Crookes visited Hughes in December 1879 and then on 20 February 1880, two more scientists came to see what was happening. The conclusion was that all the effects observed could be explained by electromagnetic induction and that nothing seen was really evidence of new waves. This was a great disappointment for Hughes and caused him to neglect further work on what he had thought, quite correctly as it turned out, to be a new phenomenon. So it was that the German scientist Heinrich Hertz instead became accepted as the discoverer of radio waves following his experiments between 1887 and 1889. The history of radio communication thus began in Britain, but as has so often been the case, the British inventor was not acknowledged and it was left to another to receive the laurels.

Seventeen years after Hughes' pioneering work in the field, a 21-year-old Italian landed in England with crates of radio equipment in which he hoped to interest the General Post Office. Unfortunately, this was at the height of the late Victorian anarchist scare, there had been several bomb attacks in the previous couple of years, and customs officers were nervous and watchful for terrorists trying to enter the country. Suspecting that the young foreigner was trying to smuggle an 'infernal device' into the country, they searched his luggage so efficiently that they destroyed his apparatus! Guglielmo Marconi was a determined character though and after settling down in the London district of Bayswater, he applied for a patent for a method relating to 'electrical actions or manifestations transmitted through air, earth or water by means of electrical oscillations of high frequency'. In June 1896, Marconi was able to secure an interview with Sir William Preece, the same man who had witnessed Hughes' demonstration. Preece was now Chief Engineer for the Post Office and he was very interested in what he saw of Marconi's work. The following year, Marconi formed the Wireless Telegraph & Signal Co. Ltd and in November 1897 the world's first permanent radio installation was set up in an hotel at Alum Bay on the Isle of Wight.

It is time to take a little excursion into the world of etymology and semantics; the meaning and derivation of words. Unless this is done, much of what follows is liable to be confusing or even incomprehensible! When we talk here about Marconi setting up a radio station, there is a natural tendency to assume that this meant the broadcasting of the human voice, which is what we generally understand today by the term 'radio'. After all, turning on the radio today means listening to people speaking or singing, or perhaps hearing music. This was not at all what was happening when Marconi established his radio station on the Isle of Wight. It would be another decade or so before the first transmission and reception of speech by this new means. What Marconi was doing was engaging in wireless telegraphy, which was another thing entirely. He was sending messages in Morse code, of the sort which were routinely sent along wires throughout the world. The only innovation in telegraphy which he was instituting was that Morse code would now be able to be received by, for instance, ships at sea.

That these early radio communication were known as 'wireless telegraphy' accounts for the word 'wireless' being used for much of the twentieth century as a synonym for 'radio'. Well, the words were not quite synonymous. Working-class people took readily to the new word 'radio' and used it freely. It was, after all, a great novelty. The upper classes however played safe and preferred to use the expression which incorporated the more familiar word 'telegraphy'. It became almost a point of honour for the well-to-do and well-educated to avoid saying 'radio', but to call it instead 'wireless'.

Educated people maintained this snobbery of using an archaic and outdated word for radio as late as the 1970s. The whole business was even codified after the Second World War, when linguist Alan Ross coined the expressions 'U' and 'Non-U' in 1954. He drew attention to the differing speech of the upper and working class. The varying accents and idioms used by the different classes had long been the object of remark, but Ross described the different vocabularies used; for example, 'looking-glass' for the upper classes and 'mirror' for the rest of the population. Nancy Mitford expanded this idea in an essay published in the magazine *Encounter*. One of the pairs of words chosen for this exercise was 'radio', which was Non-U, and 'wireless', which was U. Throughout the 1950s and beyond, those who wished to show themselves to be cultured and sophisticated made sure that they said 'wireless', rather than 'radio'.

So to begin with, radio was not at first thought of as being very much different from ordinary telegraph networks of the sort which had been familiar for over fifty years. It was only when the promise of being able to send audible speech through thin air, rather in the manner of a telephone, that the public began to be intrigued. True, there was something strange about the idea of being able to communicate, if only by Morse code, with a ship in the middle of the ocean; but although this might capture the public imagination at the time of the sinking of the *Titanic* or the attempted escape across the Atlantic of the murderous Dr Crippen, it had little bearing on everyday life.

The idea of speaking to people across the Atlantic without wires seemed so bizarre that when a company was set up in the United States to promote the development of an international radio telephone system, it ended up in court for fraud. Lee de Forest's Radio Telephone Company attracted the particular scorn of the prosecuting counsel in 1912. He told the court:

> de Forest has said in many newspapers and over his signature that it would be possible to transmit the human voice across the Atlantic before many years. Based on these absurd and deliberately misleading statements, the misguided public has been persuaded to purchase stock in his company.

The idea of transmitting the human voice around the world might indeed have seemed patently absurd to this lawyer, but it was of course the future of communications. Not for nothing did Lee de Forest later become known as the father of radio!

Talk of radio communications across the Atlantic brings us back to Marconi and his experiments in Britain. Because there was already an extensive telegraph system throughout Europe and America, in addition to a rapidly growing number of telephones, the most promising field for wireless telegraphy to exploit was marine communications, sending messages to and from ships at sea. There were several early successes in this field, but a limit on the possible usefulness of radio for this purpose was seen to be the supposed fact that radio waves would be unable to travel more than sixty or a hundred miles. This was accepted almost as dogma, because of the essential nature of electromagnetic radiation. Radio waves, like light, can travel only in straight lines. It is possible to increase the distance that such waves can travel by building higher masts, so sending them further over the horizon than is possible at ground level, but then you reach the limit imposed by the possible height of such a structure. Radio waves and light beams cannot travel far through earth and so, by this reading of the situation, the idea of sending a message by wireless telegraphy across the Atlantic Ocean must surely be a meaningless fantasy.

The value of radio at sea was proved very early in its use. A number of ships and shore stations had been equipped with Marconi's apparatus and when, on 17 March 1899, the merchant vessel *Elbe* ran aground on the Goodwin Sands, a sandbank in the English Channel, the event was witnessed by the crew of the East Goodwin Lightship. A message was sent by wireless telegraphy to the South Foreland Lighthouse, who then contacted the lifeboat at Ramsgate which at once launched a rescue mission. The following month, on 28 April, the East Goodwin Lightship was obliged to summon aid for herself, when she was rammed by the SS *R. F. Matthews*. Radio had, by the beginning of the twentieth century, proved itself very useful for ships, at least those only a few miles from the shore or each other, but there was not yet the least indication that it might grow to be a mass medium of importance or even interest to anybody other than sailors. For one thing, there was that insurmountable difficulty of sending signals more than a few miles. Marconi felt instinctively, although he had no rational basis for his belief, that this supposed limitation in sending signals was an illusion. In 1901, he set out to prove that it was possible to send a radio message 3,000 miles across the North Atlantic.

The weather in Newfoundland on 12 December 1901 was atrocious. Icy rain and gale-force winds howled around the old military hospital which stood on high ground, 600 feet above the outskirts of the capital, St John's. Almost unbelievably, somebody had chosen that day to fly a kite, which was now hovering 200 feet above the town. The previous day, observers would have seen an even stranger spectacle, when above the old hospital flew not a kite, but a balloon! There was a good and perfectly logical reason for this curious activity though, which was that Guglielmo Marconi was determined to prove that radio waves could follow the curvature of the earth's surface and were not just limited, as scientific orthodoxy claimed, to travelling in straight lines.

The purpose of the balloons and kites flying above St John's in such dreadful weather was to provide aerials in the form of trailing wires which, it was hoped, would be able to pick up signals from a transmitter in the English county of Cornwall. There, at a place called Poldhu Cove, a transmitter was sending out the letter 'S' in Morse code; just three dots repeated at intervals.

Just after noon on Wednesday, 12 December 1901, Marconi heard the signal which told him that he had been right and all the experts in the world had been wrong. Through the crackling static, he distinctly heard the three dots for which he had been listening. In his log book he laconically noted, 'Sigs at 12.30, 1.10 and 2.20'. There was controversy about the experiment and no less a person than Thomas Edison declared roundly that he didn't believe a word of it. So early in 1902, Marconi took ship from England on the *Philadelphia*, which carried a printing telegraph. Messages were received and printed out from Poldhu Cove up to 1,500 miles out at sea. The ship's captain signed the tape and the proof was now indisputable; radio could span the world.

Despite Marconi's triumph, wireless telegraphy was still an almost exclusively nautical affair when Edward VII became king in 1901. It was hard at that time to envision it as being likely to affect many people, unless they happened to be travelling by sea. This was because only brief bursts of radio waves could be sent, enough to signal dots and dashes, but certainly not steady enough to carry voices or music. This was a consequence of the way in which radio signals were generated, which was by causing sparks to jump across a gap. As this sudden burst of energy occurred, so were radio waves produced. Once again, scientific opinion was holding back progress. There was a firmly-held view that it was only by making this sudden and violent discharge that electromagnetic waves could be generated with sufficient force to travel long distances. The idea of a continuous, rolling wave, one which might be able to carry complex information upon it, was regarded as ridiculous.

Even as Marconi was limiting his work to the production of individual sparks which allowed the sending of messages in Morse code, there were others who were toying with the idea of a continuous spark or a series of sparks so rapid that they would create a rolling wave of electromagnetism. Three people were especially interested in this problem. Two of them, Lee de Forest and Valdemar Poulsen, we shall be looking at in detail in Chapter 8. The third was a man called Reginald Fessenden, a Canadian inventor who carried out most of his work in the United States.

Fessenden had various jobs, including a spell as a professor of electrical engineering. His interest in radio led him to work for the United States Weather Bureau, where he proposed setting up a chain of coastal radio stations which would be cheaper to run than those which had to be linked by telegraph wires. It was while working for the Weather Bureau and conducting experiments on Cobb Island, on the Potomac River, that Fessenden succeeded in being the first person to transmit audible and coherent speech via radio. He achieved this breakthrough on 23 December 1900, using a high-frequency spark generator, one which produced sparks so rapidly that they took on the attributes of a continuous wave, which could be used as a carrier.

A few years later, Fessenden inadvertently became the first person to transmit speech across the Atlantic. By November 1906, he had set up the National Electrical Signalling Co and was based at Brant Rock in Massachusetts. A conversation that month between Brant Rock and another station in Plymouth, also in Massachusetts, was picked up by a radio operator in Michrihanish in Scotland. Some controversy surrounds the claim that Fessenden was the first person to present a radio 'broadcast', that is to say a transmission not aimed at one specific place but intended to be heard by everybody with a receiver. Before looking at this, another excursion into the world of etymology is called for.

The word 'broadcast' is so familiar to us now, that we tend to forget that it is in fact a metaphor. With the development of seed drills in the eighteenth century, the old way of planting seed by scattering them on the ground, became less popular and eventually died out. A word was coined for this old-fashioned way of getting seeds to grow; it became known as 'broadcasting'. When wireless telegraphy began to be used for sending signals to nobody in particular, a word was needed to describe this activity and the agricultural practice of scattering seed at random seemed to be ideal for the purpose. These days, you would be hard-pressed to find anybody who understood the word 'broadcast' to relate to anything other than the sending out of electromagnetic communication which anybody can receive.

While on the subject of the derivation of the use of the word 'broadcast' in connection with radio, which of course occurred before the First World War, it is not generally known that some years later there was an attempt to coin an analogous expression for the act of listening in to a broadcast! In the 1920s the British Broadcasting Corporation held a competition to find just such a word. The winner was 'broadcatch', as in, 'I shall broadcatch the news tonight'. Alas, it never caught on, although the term was revived in the 1980s for use in a digital context.

There are at least two rival claimants for the distinction of having been the first person to give a public broadcast, aimed at all and sundry and with no greater purpose than entertaining those listening in. Most books today give the date of the world's first radio broadcast as being Christmas Eve, 1906. It was on this day that Reginald Fessenden supposedly played the violin, read a few verses from the Bible and then finished off by playing a gramophone record. The story is that this took place at his radio station in Brant Rock Massachusetts and the broadcast was picked up by ships at sea. Unfortunately, the earliest account of this broadcast did not appear until 1932, by which time Fessenden had died. Extensive research over the years has failed to uncover any kind of corroborating evidence. There is no record of it in ships' logs, no contemporary witnesses or anybody who remembered the actual event. The safest verdict on the matter must therefore be the old Scottish one of 'Not Proven'.

No such uncertainty attaches itself to the first British broadcast of both music and speech. It took place from a Royal Navy cruiser, HMS *Andromeda*, in 1907. The ship was moored on the Thames off Chatham, and Lieutenant Quentin Crauford obtained permission from his superiors to stage and broadcast a concert party on board her. The Admiralty were not being entirely benevolent and easy-going when they made the decision to allow this bit of fun. Lieutenant Crauford had made his own adaptations to the wireless telegraphy transmitter on the ship and wished to test out his belief that it was now capable of sending more than just the dots and dashes necessary to pass a message in Morse. There were of course military implications if Crauford was right about this; the navy were particularly intrigued by the possibility that it might be possible to communicate with submarines using this new transmitter. A condition of the party going ahead was therefore that it was to remain secret. In Lieutenant Crauford's own words:

> In 1907 I had several signalmen to help me. I chose the most musical of them to sing the first song, 'God Save the King'. This was the first song ever broadcast. We followed it up with 'Rule Britannia', 'Trafalgar Day', 'On the Mississippi Shore', 'There is a Tavern in the Town', 'Three Blind Mice' and others.

This very British collection of songs, interspersed with Crauford's commentary, ranks as the first definite instance of music being broadcast for entertainment.

The same year that the concert party took place on HMS *Andromeda*, the first regular broadcasts began in America. The De Forest Radio Telephone Co set up a studio on the top floor of the Parker Building, on New York's Fourth Avenue. From there, Lee de Forest began to play gramophone records over the air, for anybody with a radio set to pick up. He wrote in his diary: 'My present task (happy one) is to distribute sweet melody broadcast over the city and sea so that in time even the mariner far out across the silent waves may hear the music of his homeland.' This provides us, incidentally, with a very early example of the word 'broadcast' being used. It will be noted that de Forest uses the word as an adverb, saying that he will distribute sweet melody 'broadcast'. It took a few years for the use of the term to settle down until it was used only as a noun or verb.

Within two years, Lee de Forest had expanded the operation of his radio station and was inviting people into the studio and interviewing them live on air. In 1909, he spoke on air to his mother-in-law, the well-known suffragist

Harriet Stanton Blatch. The following year saw another first – the world's first outside broadcast.

On 13 January 1910, the great Enrico Caruso was starring at the Metropolitan Opera House in New York. The operas were *Cavellaria Rusticana* and *Pagliacci*. The De Forest Radio Telephone Co had secured the cooperation of the opera house to transmit the performance that evening live to anybody able to tune into it. Some receivers were already turned on and waiting, for example at the Metropolitan Life Building and also at the Hotel Breslin, near Times Square. In New York harbour, the captain of RMS *Avon* had invited over 200 guests to listen to the opera on board his ship. Nothing of the sort had ever been attempted before and the novelty of being able to hear Caruso singing without being anywhere near the opera house was an irresistible draw. Everything went smoothly and the broadcast was picked up all over the city by various people, including radio operators at the Brooklyn Navy Yard.

It is interesting to note that Caruso's very presence at the Metropolitan Opera House was a direct consequence of another development in the field of analogue communications. We sometimes forget that the word 'gramophone' is not a generic term but rather a trade name for the machine developed by Emile Berliner in the late 1880s. Just as we often call any vacuum cleaner a 'Hoover', so too did the name 'gramophone' come to be used for any device playing flat records; as opposed to the cylinders produced by Thomas Edison's company. There was for the next fifteen years a format war between the two systems, each trying to show its superiority to the other. As part of this commercial struggle, Berliner's Gramophone Co. had been trying to lure well-known names to record for them.

In April 1903, composer Edvard Grieg was induced to visit the Paris recording studio of the Gramophone Co and play some of his piano pieces. This was a real coup, which was followed that same year by the recording of an entire opera. Verdi's *Ernani* was released on a set of forty single-sided, ten-inch discs. The year before, the 29-year-old Caruso had also been persuaded to record some gramophone records, for which he was paid £100. The ten records became bestsellers in Europe and even found their way across the Atlantic. Heinrich Conreid of New York's Metropolitan Opera House happened to hear one of these records and instantly decided that he had to have the young singer for his own establishment. He wired Caruso and offered him a firm engagement, based only upon the record he had heard, the first time that such a thing had ever happened. When Caruso opened at the Metropolitan on 23

November 1903, it was the beginning of a long and fruitful association, which would almost certainly never have come about had it not been for the technological innovations which were now sweeping through the Western World.

Returning now to radio, we recall that there were already long-distance electrical communications, both in Britain and America, at that time. The telegraph network spanned Europe and North America and the telephone had been a familiar fact of life for many years. This, however, was something quite different. Contact with friends, acquaintances and business contacts via these media were generally brief and invariably conducted on a one-to-one basis. This, on the other hand, was an anonymous means of communication with complete strangers. It was an utterly new and, for most people, very strange concept.

It is important once again to stress the distinction which existed in early radio between wireless telegraphy and what was known then as radio telephony. Wireless telegraphy, the sending of Morse code by radio rather than through wires, was not all that different from ordinary telegraphy. It is true that the idea of those messages passing invisibly through the air to their destination was an odd one and the public were eager to hear about some of the remarkable things which wireless telegraphs achieved. Radio telephony though, the transmission of speech, was in another league entirely. It might be called telephony, but of course this was not like speaking to somebody on the telephone. As the news spread of things like the broadcasting of an entire opera in New York, it became clear that whatever the name of the company undertaking such marvels, in this case the De Forest Radio Telephone Co, this really had no association at all with chatting on the telephone. It seemed to be a one-way process, for one thing, with people listening in, but unable to respond. In other words, it was an entirely passive business, perhaps in some ways like a visit to the cinema.

Just like the early adopters of computers, with their wires and aerials and jury-rigged modems, so too with the first radio enthusiasts. Something exciting was going on and they wanted to be a part of it. It was known by 1906 that messages in Morse could cross the Atlantic, so what was to stop somebody in possession of a radio receiver becoming connected with the whole world? The seemingly insuperable difficulty was that radios at that time were enormously complicated and expensive. It might be possible for an ocean liner crossing to America to be able to afford such a thing, but they were beyond the reach of the ordinary hobbyist. This changed abruptly on 30 August 1906, when an American who rejoiced in the peculiar Christian name of 'Greenleaf' filed a patent in the United States. It could hardly have been for a duller subject, a silicon crystal detector, and yet Greenleaf Whittier Pickard's invention was to make radio accessible to the masses. Wireless telegraphy and radio telephony were about to move into the domestic sphere; both in Britain and the United States.

The element silicon has played an important part in the digital revolution which has transformed our lives since the 1980s. Its use as a semiconductor has made possible all those technological gadgets upon which we rely so heavily. It also played a vital role in the earlier Analogue Revolution at which we are looking. After experimenting with over 30,000 combinations of various materials, Greenleaf Pickard found that silicon was ideal for what he had in mind. He was looking for a simple and cheap way to detect and listen to radio signals. With a long piece of wire to act as an aerial, all that was needed was a crystal of silicon with a very thin wire resting against it. This fine wire gave rise to the other name by which such receivers became known – 'cat's whisker' sets.

Essentially, those early crystal radios, built along the lines suggested in Pickard's patent, which was granted three months after he applied for it, were made of very little other than the aerial and silicon crystal. The principle behind them was very simple. Radio waves striking the aerial caused a slight electric current to flow through it. This passed through a coil, which filtered it and then to the crystal detector, where it was demodulated. An earphone was needed to hear the signals which were picked up, but that was pretty much it. The crystal radio, though, was very significant for two reasons. In the first place, it allowed anybody to start tinkering with radio and eavesdropping on the world. Messages from ships to ports could be received, sometimes experimental broadcasts from other countries. Listening to 'cat's whisker' sets of this sort became a popular hobby. Secondly, it was a harbinger of the age of electronics; although this did not become apparent for many years.

Lee de Forest's triode, his Audion vacuum tube, appeared in the same year that Greenleaf Pickard's crystal radio was patented. It is a debatable point which of these two innovations was the first electronic device. Together, they ushered in a new age; the age of electronics. The crystal radio, with its piece of metal pressed against a piece of silicon, was the first instance of a semiconductor diode.

We end this chapter with two final examples of the way in which radio was changing, and indeed shaping, the world during the Edwardian period. We are so familiar with the Eiffel Tower as representing Paris and, by extension, France, that it is difficult to imagine that at one time this iconic structure was widely loathed, with many people campaigning for its demolition. When construction of the Eiffel Tower began in 1887, 300 prominent artists and writers signed a letter to the newspaper *Le Temps*, denouncing the project. Signatories, including Guy de Maupassant and Charles Gounod, described,

> a giddy, ridiculous tower dominating Paris like a gigantic black smokestack, crushing under its barbaric bulk Notre Dame, the Tour Saint-Jacques, the Louvre, the dome of Les Invalides, the Arc de Triomphe, all of our humiliated monuments will disappear in this ghastly dream.

Since Eiffel had only been given a permit for the building for twenty years, dating from the World's Fair held in Paris in 1889, there was an excellent chance that at the end of that time, the authorities would simply order him to dismantle the thing. To prevent this happening, Gustave Eiffel decided to make his tower indispensable to the scientific community. Because it was the tallest building in the world, at 300 metres high, it was useful for measuring the difference in air pressure at ground level and the top of the tower. Eiffel also demonstrated wind resistance and even built a wind tunnel at the base of his tower. It was radio, though, which really made the Eiffel Tower vital to France both as a military asset and also a matter of international prestige.

In 1903, Eiffel invited the French army to use his tower, which proved a success. The sheer height of the thing made it possible for the French officer who was stationed at the Eiffel Tower to make contact with every fort in France. By 1908, signals were being exchanged with military bases in the French North African colony of Morocco. But it was when the tower's radio station became involved with international timekeeping that the future of the Eiffel Tower was really assured.

We are so used to being able accurately to establish the precise time that this is taken for granted. One need only glance at any computer screen or mobile telephone to see exactly what time it is. Even thirty years ago though, matters were very different. In the 1980s, anybody wishing to be sure of the right time would either need to telephone the Speaking Clock or, more likely, tune into the BBC at certain key times, in order to listen to the time signal which preceded news broadcasts, the famous Greenwich 'pips'. The time signal from Greenwich had its origins in what was being done at the Eiffel Tower and is a curious and interesting story in itself.

For almost the whole of human history, there has been no way of determining the correct time, other than by looking at the sky and seeing where the sun or stars are. Even as late as the start of the Industrial Revolution in the eighteenth century, work began at dawn and the midday meal was perhaps eaten when the sun was at its highest point. There is no real need for accurate timekeeping in agriculture; nothing much happens in a field of wheat in the course of an hour. The cycle on farms is geared to the rising and setting of the sun and, in the longer term, to the seasons. With the coming of industrialization, all this changed. Factory shifts started at definite and specific hours and the ability to be at work on time was suddenly vital. As railway trains and steamships became more and more common, timekeeping assumed an even greater importance.

In the late nineteenth century, almost all clocks were mechanical and generally needed to be put right at least once or twice a week. This could prove tricky, because whatever clock you used to check your own watch or clock against was also an unreliable mechanical device which might not itself be correct. There were very accurate timepieces, but these tended to be in observatories such as the one at Greenwich. There was certainly no way of checking your own clock against the one at Greenwich, unless you happened to be in London. This lack of precision could quite literally be a matter of life and death.

On 18 April 1891, two railway trains approached Kipton, a village in the American state of Ohio. They were due to reach a junction, one after the other, with a gap of four minutes between them. Unfortunately, the watch belonging to the engineer on one of the trains was faulty and stopped for a few minutes, before starting again. The result was that the drivers of both trains believed themselves to be on time and so both arrived simultaneously at Kipton Junction. Nine people died in the train wreck which followed. The tragedy spurred both the development of cheap and reliable pocket watches, as well as the search for an infallible way of checking the correct time.

In most countries of the early twentieth century, there were only one or two locations where one could be absolutely sure of finding out the exact time. In England, for instance, the Royal Observatory at Greenwich was one such place. A ball was dropped down a pole at precisely 1.00 pm and Londoners could set their watches and clocks by this. The Paris Observatory fulfilled a similar function, as the arbiter of correct time. As telephones became more common, the Paris Observatory was frequently called by people wishing to know the right time, so that they could set their watches and clocks. This eventually became such a nuisance that it led to the introduction of the world's first speaking clock, but before then the observatory found a way of cutting down on the numbers of people who telephoned them, by teaming up with Eiffel and broadcasting a time signal from the top of the Eiffel

Tower, from where it would be picked up not only in the whole of France, but even across the Channel in England.

Broadcasting of the radio signal from the Eiffel Tower, which indicated the time within a fraction of a second, began in 1910. All across Europe and even out to sea, people began to tune into the Paris radio station to set their clocks, confident in the knowledge that the time was completely correct. It will come as little or no surprise to learn that after this coup, when the twenty-year permit for the Eiffel Tower expired, there was no question of anybody ordering it to be taken down. Instead, the municipal authorities in Paris granted another lease, this time one of seventy years.

The famous Greenwich 'pips' on the radio originated indirectly from the time signals transmitted from the Eiffel Tower. In 1895, a British company called Synchronome Ltd was set up in London. It was run by a man called Frank Hope-Jones and the idea was that the company would manufacture extremely accurate electric clocks; consisting of a 'master', connected electrically to a number of 'slaves'. By this means, a factory or school could ensure that all its clocks were synchronized to one standard. Even better; there was no need for somebody to go around the premises laboriously winding the clocks every day and setting them right. In 1913, the Synchronome company branched out into the field of radio. They began to produce a crystal set which was designed to pick up the time signals from the Eiffel Tower. This meant that anybody would be able to adjust clocks and watches to the greatest accuracy of the day.

The Horophone, which is what the crystal radio made by Synchronome was called, proved quite a success. Not only was a time signal being sent from the Eiffel Tower, but also weather forecasts and news bulletins, all in Morse code rather than by the human voice. Factories and other businesses which wished to be up-to-date and modern purchased the Horophone and set their clocks by it. The idea of being able to find out the correct time by radio was seen as being the epitome of modernity.

In April 1923 Hope-Jones was invited by the newly-formed British Broadcasting Company to give a radio talk about British Summer Time. Immediately after this broadcast, Hope-Jones suggested to the technicians in the studio that they might consider broadcasting a time signal, consisting of a several 'pips', one which enable people to know the exact time each day. After discussions with the Astronomer Royal,

Frank Dyson, the idea was approved and the first Greenwich 'pips' were broadcast in February 1924.

The sound of the time signal from Greenwich was to become a familiar one in almost every home in the country; in the morning, it would enable people to know whether they were on time for getting to work and so on. The slow infiltration of analogue technology into people's homes though began at least twenty years before the first 'pips' broadcast by the BBC. We have looked at the mass media which were revolutionizing life, perhaps we should see how the information revolution was changing the domestic scene, as various aspects of it became a fixed part of family life in Edwardian Britain.

Chapter 6

The Analogue Revolution at Home

Edwardian society was without doubt being shaped and moulded by the advances in communication and the copying and storage of information. Change was also taking place rapidly on the domestic front too, as homes began to be invaded by both new inventions and radical improvements to familiar devices. The best way of seeing how the adoption and widespread use of analogue technology suddenly exploded after the turn of the nineteenth century is to look first at one specific instance. Let us consider photographic cameras, a simple example of a piece of machinery designed to make analogue copies, in this case visual images of people, buildings, scenery and anything else one wishes to capture and make permanent.

The first photographs were taken in the third decade of the nineteenth century, so by 1900 the process had been around for over seventy years. For most of that time, the production of photographs with a camera was an exceedingly time-consuming and complicated process. Take the so-called 'wet collodion' method, popular among amateur photographers in the 1850s. A scrupulously clean glass plate, typically measuring eight by ten inches, first had to be carefully polished. A solution of guncotton dissolved in ether, the collodion, then had to be prepared. It was necessary to pour this swiftly and evenly over the whole surface of the glass plate. One needed to work fast, because the solution dried quickly and the photograph had to be exposed while the collodion was still wet. The plate then had to be dipped, and so sensitised, in a bath of silver nitrate.

Throughout the whole of the above operation, it was essential that the wet plate was not smudged and that not so much as a speck of dust or dirt allowed to settle on the surface. The chemicals had to be at just the right temperature and the concentrations within very narrow parameters. Rushing to place the wet plate into the camera, the photograph could now be taken. Landscapes were easy enough to take, people not so much. An exposure time of about forty-five seconds was needed with this method. We sometimes have the idea that the Victorians were a po-faced and humourless bunch, because in all the photographs from that time they are staring straight at the camera with fixed expressions on their faces; often they are frowning grimly. The reason for this is simple. It is very difficult to hold a smile for more than a couple of seconds, before it begins to look like a frozen rictus. If you're going to hold an expression for almost a minute, it is much less awkward to relax the face entirely, which can lend even the most cheerful and good-natured of men a forbidding air. Illustration 10 shows Charles Darwin, an amiable-enough chap in real life, looking furiously angry as he strives to keep his face immobile for half a minute or so. Fixing and developing pictures was also a performance entailing the use of baths of chemicals, which once again had to be precisely the right potency and correct temperature.

Photography was an expensive, middle-class hobby for the Victorians and it is hardly to be wondered at that when taking each picture involved so much fuss and bother, the Victorian photographer preferred to take portraits of his family and friends, who of course belonged, like him, to a certain stratum of society. Which in turn accounts for the fact that the majority of the people one sees in photographs of this time are respectable and well-dressed men and women rather than street urchins. Our ideas about society in those days have been heavily influenced by the complexity and financial cost of the means used to record it.

Throughout the nineteenth century, the cost of photography as a hobby fell and it simultaneously grew simpler, until all that was necessary was to point a camera pre-loaded with film and press the shutter. This stage had been reached as early as 1888, when George Eastman in America founded the Kodak company. His cameras were sold under the advertising slogan 'You press the button, we do the rest'. This was no idle boast. The camera, with the film inside it, was returned to the manufacturer, who then undertook to develop and print the photographs for the customer.

The real revolution in photography began almost precisely as the new century dawned. In February 1900, the Eastman Kodak company put on the market a new type of camera which showed just how far things had come in the years since the wet collodion technique had been popular. The 'Brownie' camera was nothing more than a stout cardboard box with a lens and mechanical shutter. It used rolls of film rather than plates and took square pictures a little over two inches wide. Perhaps the most radical feature of the new camera was the price; it retailed in the United States for just $1. In Britain, the 'Brownie' was priced at five shillings, 25p in today's currency. It may be seen in Illustration 11, held by the eponymous Brownie after whom it was named.

Because it had been designed by an employee of Kodak called Frank Brownell, in later years a little bit of folk etymology arose, to the effect that the Brownie camera had been named after a diminutive form of the inventor's name. The true origin of the world's most famous, some say most important, camera is more interesting than that. Throughout the 1890s, there could be few people in the United States who had not encountered the images of Brownies dreamed up by a Canadian artist called Palmer Cox. Just as today, we are all of us familiar with the figures of Disney characters such as Elsa from *Frozen* or Belle from *Beauty and the Beast*, so too were Palmer Cox's Brownies universally recognized. They featured in strip cartoons in a Sunday newspaper and also in a series of books. Palmer Cox's Brownies became so popular that they appeared on all kinds of merchandise, from calendars and cigars to children's games. Using them to promote a new type of camera was an inspired, if somewhat underhand, move on the part of George Eastman, the owner of the Eastman Kodak company. Why underhand? There is no record of Palmer Cox ever having been acknowledged in any way by Kodak, nor receiving any payment for the use of his famous creation to market the Brownie camera.

It was not only the name of 'Brownie' which launched the world's most famous camera, the visual image was also used. It sometimes seems that we believe subconsciously that the distant past was a pretty colourless and anaemic place. All those white statues and columns in ancient Greece and Rome, the dreary grey stone of medieval cathedrals: did people in the past not have our modern appreciation of vibrant colours? Of course they did. Those Greek statues were originally painted in lifelike tones, but the paint has flaked off over the centuries. Similarly, cathedrals too were riots of colour in the sixteenth century, with the various tombs bright with primary colours and gold leaf. Just like the statues of antiquity, the colours have worn and faded, leaving us with a monochrome or sepia-tinted view of the past! Looking at those old Brownies now, we see only drab little black boxes, but of course when they were sold, those cameras were as bright as any modern product. A cardboard sleeve enclosed the camera, covered with garish images of the eponymous Brownies, each wielding a camera. This familiar image attracted young and old alike. Everybody knew the Brownies!

The 'Brownie' ushered in the age of popular photography, a camera so simple that children could, and did, use it. Instead of starchy groups of upper middle-class Victorians sitting and gazing straight ahead, their faces blank and expressionless, from 1900 onwards we have thousands of unposed pictures of all sorts and conditions of people at work and play, often unaware that they were being photographed and recorded for posterity.

In short, cameras had been available for well over fifty years before the dawn of the Edwardian era: there was nothing novel about photography. What *was* new was the introduction of small, cheap cameras with exposure times of a fraction of a second. No bulky equipment was needed, no bottles of developer, no black cloth for the photographer to cover himself with as he focused the image; not even a tripod was necessary. The age of the 'snapshot' had dawned.

Although there are just as many posed portraits of important citizens from the Edwardian years as there are from the nineteenth century, the photographic record of those times contains something else. Higher shutter speeds and the proliferation of cameras which could be carried about on holidays, days out or even just while strolling in the streets, mean that there are any number of candid and natural pictures from the years leading up to the First World War, photographs which show all sorts of men, women and children at home, enjoying themselves at the seaside, playing in parks or just living their day-to-day lives. These people are not sitting bolt upright and staring straight ahead with a fixed look upon their faces. Instead, they are walking, running, playing sports, splashing in the sea or dancing around a maypole. It is as though the waxwork figures who seemingly inhabited Victorian Britain have come suddenly to life!

This democratisation of photography marks the beginning of modern history. We rely upon Charles Dickens to tell us what life was like in the working-class districts of London, but from 1900 onwards, we can see for ourselves what life in such places was like. We can see children playing in the streets and even peep inside the houses and look at the living conditions to be found there. We no longer need some middle-class novelist or philanthropist to select the points to which he feels our attention should be drawn; working people show us what they themselves thought worth recording.

Cheap cameras were one innovation in photography which arrived in the early years of the twentieth century. There was another, one of which many people are unaware. This was the first widely-available commercial colour film. Curiously, the introduction of colour photography, while rendering the images of people and scenes with great vividness and startling realism, also slowed down the process of photography and returned it in a way to the style that which existed half a century earlier. This paradox deserves a little explanation.

More sensitive black-and-white film meant, as a matter of course, faster shutter speeds. This accounts for the informal nature of many Edwardian photographs, when compared with those taken during the nineteenth century. When you work with an exposure time of thirty seconds, then obviously, your subject must remain perfectly still. If, on the other hand, you have a shutter speed of a thirtieth, or even a sixtieth, of a second, this will mean an exposure time of perhaps a thousandth as long. It doesn't matter if somebody is sitting down or standing up; they can even be walking down the street and the shutter will freeze the action. When looking at black-and-white photographs taken by Edwardians, one has the feeling that people have started moving and they are no longer posed like static tableaux in a waxworks museum. This process of coming to life was influenced by the development of actual moving pictures in the 1890s.

The Lumière brothers, Louis and Auguste, were instrumental in the creation of cinema. In 1895, they perfected the cinematograph projector, the first device which actually projected moving films on a screen. Eadweard Muybridge had projected photographic images years earlier, but these had merely been a continuous repetition of individual photographs. It is the Lumières whom we must thank for first showing actual films to the world.

The two brothers were intrigued not only by the idea of producing moving pictures, at which they were very successful, but also by the possibility of a process of colour photography which could be widely exploited and would require no specialized equipment. It will be remembered that the first colour photograph of all required three projectors operating in a darkened room. There were other attempts in the late nineteenth century at taking pictures in colour, but none of the systems with which people experimented were simple and straightforward. The Lumières dreamed of allowing people to take colour photographs as easily as they were currently doing in black-and-white. On 10 June 1907, the two brothers demonstrated the results of this quest in Paris, before an audience of 600 people. They called their process 'autochrome' and it is no exaggeration to say that it revolutionized photography.

In some ways autochrome was a step backwards in photography. In the first place, it required the use of specially-treated glass plates, rather than convenient rolls of celluloid film. This made the taking of pictures a little cumbersome, because the cameras needed for these plates were bulky and required tripods. Autochrome also produced direct positives, which meant that each photograph was unique and could not be endlessly reproduced, as was the case when negatives were made in the camera and positive prints made from these. Every autochrome shot was a one-off. Finally, these plates needed a much longer exposure time than the black-and-white films which were being widely used by 1907. In bright sunlight, the shutter had to remain open for two or three seconds, several times as long on an overcast and cloudy day. All this meant that human subjects had to maintain their position for at least a few seconds, which had in the nineteenth century resulted in so many stilted and obviously posed portraits.

It was ironic that the Lumière brothers, who had helped bring the world to life with their cinematograph, should now cause it to slow down again dramatically, by increasing the exposure time for their new photographs to what it had been forty years earlier. However, there was a subtle difference in the pictures which were now taken with this new method.

Times had changed since the days of the Victorian portrait and so those holding a pose for seconds at a time were no longer wearing their best and most formal clothes, while sitting upright and frowning. The people captured in autochrome shots look quite different. It is as though a game of musical statues was being played and all those people who had come to life in moving pictures and action shots taken with fast shutters and sensitive film were suddenly frozen again in new and more naturalistic poses. Photographed Victorian authors are serious and respectable, looking in the main as though they have just come from a grand function. They are dressed as though about to deliver a lecture or attend a dinner party. Consider, by way of contrast, one of the last photographs ever taken of American author Mark Twain. It may be seen in Illustration 12.

Although this black-and-white image does not allow us to appreciate the rich colours of the autochrome, in particular the red dressing gown which Twain was wearing, we can see that he slumps in his bed, not even facing the camera. Not only is he not wearing a tie, he is dressed for the bedroom rather than the salon. The whole air of this picture is one of relaxed indifference to the camera. It is as though he has been caught unawares in a private moment. Other autochromes from the time reveal a similarly 'laid-back' air. A teenage girl is seen wearing a scarlet bathing dress and lounging casually on a beach, leaning against a boat. The autochrome was especially successful with the colour red, which explains why so many of these old photographs make use of red clothing. Red and auburn hair too comes out very well in this process. Like the Pre-Raphaelites, autochrome photographers were very keen on red hair. The playwright George Bernard Shaw was an early adopter of autochrome and he and a friend took pictures of each other in the autumn of 1907. Shaw's ginger beard came out with particular vividness!

Some of the most famous autochromes from the early days of colour photography are of women with red hair, some of which really do put one in mind of the work of artists such as Rossetti. In America Paul Burty Haviland took many pictures of Florence Peterson, a teenage girl with flaming red hair. She was photographed in various poses, including without any clothes on. Austrian Heinrich Kuhn worked in autochrome and his photographs have been described as the most beautiful ever taken using this system. Perhaps the best portrait shows Kuhn's children Lotte and Hans in 1912. They are featured in a group with their governess, Mary Warner. What is most striking about this picture is that Warner's face is wholly obscured: she is looking down at the youngest child. All we can see is the top of her head, which shows to great advantage the masses of red hair which she has coiled up. It is such images which show autochrome at its best.

The heyday of autochrome was the years before the First World War, when colour photography was frankly a novelty. There is something a little disconcerting about seeing the vivid colour photographs taken at that time; a period which for most of us can only be visualized in black-and-white. It was to be many years before colour photography really took off, but these early photographs show us that over a century ago, people still had the same desire for bright colours and gaudy decoration which we have today.

Over the last twenty-five years or so, and particularly since the beginning of the new millennium, communications in this country have been revolutionized. Until the 1990s, anybody wishing to keep in touch with relatives or friends would primarily do so through the spoken word, either in the course of face-to-face conversations or through talking on the telephone. Contact with those who lived a long way away might sometimes be maintained by writing and receiving letters, but this had grown relatively rare by the end of the twentieth century. Most people simply spoke to each other to make arrangements or just to keep in touch or chat. This has changed, and the written word is now used far more for everyday contact than talking. Many young people communicate with their friends almost exclusively by typing text into electronic devices.

This trend towards the use of typed, rather than spoken, words to communicate with each other has seen a proliferation of visual images used to accompany, illustrate and enliven the text. Cartoons, snapshots, pictures of kittens or celebrities, photographs with amusing or witty captions and any number of memes; the list is endless. These images pad out a short text message or comment on Facebook or Snapchat and make it look more visually attractive. Pictures are not infrequently adapted, by the addition of text superimposed over the original image. Emoticons add an extra visual dimension. All this means that there are two chief features of modern, demotic communication and social interaction in Britain and other industrialized nations. The first of these is that it is multimodal, that is to say, it consists not just of one medium but at least two. Sometimes, audio files or clips of film are also attached to the message. Words are combined with photographs, cartoons or other visual aids in to get across or emphasise a message. The second and perhaps more prominent feature of the way in which people today keep in touch is the immediacy of the thing. Messages are sent and received almost instantaneously. Nobody these days wishes to hang about, waiting for letters or even telephone calls. They need to know that their words have been seen almost as soon as they have been sent.

This rapidity of day-to-day communication lends the modern age an air of increasing, some might say frenetic, speed. In the time which it might once have taken to write a letter, an entire conversation may well have taken place today, enlivened perhaps with pictures or sound. We are, we feel, more 'connected' with our families and friends than ever before. Every trifling aspect of our lives can now be shared with others with hardly a thought being given to the process.

Readers might be more than a little surprised to learn that the Edwardians were every bit as keen on keeping in touch with their friends in this way as are the millennials and so-called 'digital natives' who currently embrace pictures and print as a way of keeping in touch, in preference to actually speaking! The medium used at the beginning of the twentieth century, a by-product of the increasing sophistication of printing processes at which we have looked, was the picture postcard.

The sending of postcards in this country has declined dramatically in recent years and is now limited to the occasional card sent from seaside resorts. Most young people would not dream of sending a postcard, feeling that a brief film from their mobile, accompanied by a few typed words of explanation, more than fits the bill instead. The situation in Edwardian Britain could hardly have been more different. Few people had telephones in their homes and letter writing was too formal and stiff for day-to-day needs. The postcard was the easiest and most convenient method of contacting one's acquaintances, if it was not possible to visit them in person. More than that, it was the chosen way to contact people throughout the day, much as we now text somebody or use instant messaging to let them know what is going on. A brief look at the origins of the postcard and its use in Britain will serve to put this in context.

The first postcards in Britain had no pictures on them. They were just plain cards; one side of which was for the address and the other side for the message. They first went on sale on 1 October 1870 and were produced and sold by the Post Office. Each card cost just a halfpenny; half the price of the cost of sending an ordinary letter. In the first week that they went on sale, a million were sold. The new medium of communication incorporated an impressed halfpenny stamp and were sold for that amount; just the cost of the stamp. This, in itself, made them at once very attractive to working people. Until then, anybody wishing to send a letter had to buy paper and envelopes and then pay 1d for a stamp. Now, all that was needed was to spend half the cost of the standard stamp and your message would be delivered within a few hours.

From the very beginning there was a feeling that postcards were a vulgar means of sending a message and respectable people shunned them. It was thought that there was something almost indecent about writing a brief letter that anybody at all could see, rather than shrouding it in an envelope. Why, even the postman could read what you had to say, if he felt inclined to read it! This touches upon an interesting point, in that postcards, even when sent to members of your own family, were essentially public communications. Several libel cases were launched which began with the sending of postcards which had been read by people other than the intended recipient. Just as posting a comment on Facebook is recognized to be a public statement, so too with postcards. Whatever you wrote was deemed by the law to enter the public domain as soon as it was posted. The parallels between the sending of postcards and posting comments today on social media are quite striking.

The acceptance of the postcard as a means of sending brief messages was largely the doing of Prime Minister William Gladstone, who took to the new medium with great enthusiasm. He sent hundreds of postcards and almost single-handedly turned it into a respectable way to keep in touch. By the end of the nineteenth century, postcards were more or less accepted by most people as a cheap and convenient alternative to sending a telegram. Sending a telegram in late Victorian Britain cost a penny a word, which meant that one had to be reasonably prosperous to use this service. In the comic novel *The Diary of a Nobody*, published in 1892, the protagonist has occasion to send a telegram to an acquaintance, accepting an invitation to dinner, and writes in his diary:

> As he had said nothing about dress in the letter, I wired back: 'With pleasure. Is it full dress?' and by leaving out our name, just got the message within the sixpence.

1. The photophone. The origin of fibre-optic cables: telephone calls transmitted along beams of light.

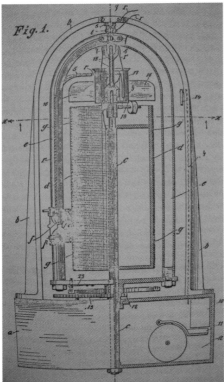

2. Patent design for the telegraphone. Computer hard drives have their origins in this Edwardian technology.

3. Edwardian Britain as it is now remembered. Grand ladies carrying parasols attend 'Glorious Goodwood' during the high-water mark of the Empire.

4. The Code of Hammurabi. The invention of writing, the first information revolution, marked the beginning of both history and civilization.

5. An early printing press. The second information revolution was triggered by the invention of moveable type; the Reformation was a by-product of the spread of printing.

6. A steam rotary press at the *Times*. The third information revolution coincided with the Industrial Revolution.

7. A hand-coloured stereoscopic Daguerreotype. Each new development in information and communication technology will be used for surprising and unexpected purposes.

8. The keyboard of a Linotype printing press. This particular machine was in use for almost a century, between 1888 and 1980

9. The storming of the Winter Palace. Fake news from over a century ago.

10. A formal portrait from Victorian Britain. The lengthy exposure time meant that subjects had to remain perfectly still for half a minute, often lending them a grim and forbidding air.

11. The Brownie after whom the Box Brownie was named. The arrival of cheap cameras allowed ordinary people to chronicle their lives.

12. Autochrome photograph of Mark Twain. Compare the relaxed informality of this portrait with the one of Charles Darwin in Illustration 10, taken fifty years earlier.

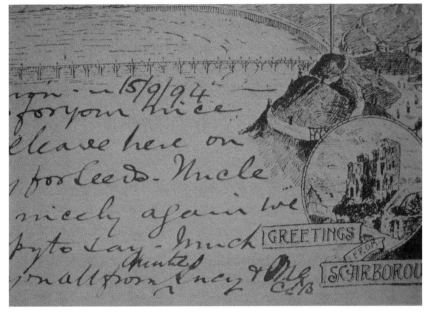

13. The first picture postcard printed in Britain. Note that because the address takes up the whole of one side, the message has been written on the picture side.

14. A postcard showing the iconic horn of an early phonograph. The child dosing the machine with Beecham's Pills is a comment upon the quality of sound from such contraptions!

Mr Caudle unable to stand Mrs Caudle's tongue any longer, goes and sleeps with the children.

15. A humorous picture postcard from 1907.

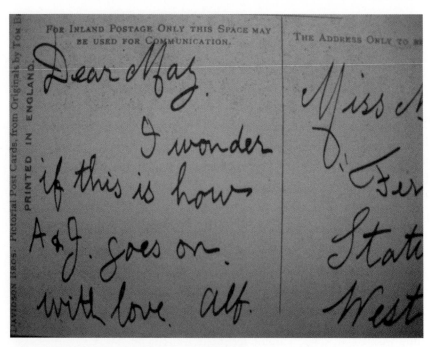

16. A brief message referring to the picture shown in Illustration 15.

17. A 'typewriting operative'. This was one of the new careers brought about by the Edwardian information revolution, which enabled well-brought-up girls to go out to work, while remaining respectable.

18. A telephone exchange at the turn of the century. It is staffed entirely by young women, who were thought to be more reliable and less troublesome than boys.

19. An 'instant' camera which delivers prints within a minute. This futuristic device dates from before the First World War.

20. A Photostat machine from 1912. These were being installed in public libraries before 1914.

For the same price, Mr Pooter might have sent a dozen postcards!

It was the advent of the picture postcard which really precipitated the postcard's meteoric rise and caused it to become the people's choice for everyday communication of all kinds. The first authenticated example of a British picture postcard is one bearing a crude line representation of the coastal resort of Scarborough in Yorkshire; which was posted on 15 September 1894. It may be seen in Illustration 13.

The picture postcard was at first slow to catch on. There were two reasons for this. In the first place, the manufacturers and sellers of the things insisted that they be sold only in packs of six, a short-sighted policy designed to increase sales, which had in fact the opposite effect. The second factor which prevented this sort of postcard from becoming immediately popular was a Post Office regulation which stipulated that one side of the card could bear nothing but the address, which of course meant that any picture or illustration could not take up an entire side of the card, but had to be shared with the written message. It will be observed in Illustration 13 that the sender has been obliged to write the message across the picture itself.

In 1901, a German printer called Hartmann wished to start manufacturing picture postcards in Britain, but did not want to do so unless he could cover the whole of one side with a brightly-coloured picture. We are so used today to the convention that the back of a postcard is divided in two, with half for the address and half for the message, that it is hard to grasp how radical this proposal was at the time. It was an idea whose time had come and the Postmaster-General not only gave his permission for the enterprise to go ahead and the rules to be relaxed, but he also wrote to the editor of *Picture Postcard Magazine* and asked him to publish a statement to this effect, which duly appeared in the January 1902 edition. That there was, as early as 1902, a magazine devoted solely to picture postcards is an indication of just how popular they were becoming at this time. Collecting postcards, both those received in the post and others purchased for the sake of it, was fast becoming a craze. Special albums were sold so that people's collections of postcards could be more easily displayed.

The decision to allow pictures to occupy the whole of one side of a postcard opened the floodgates. The new printing techniques, at which we have already looked, combined with the availability of cheap paper and bright, colourful inks meant that the age of the picture postcard was about to dawn. Just one single statistic will perhaps leave readers gaping with astonishment. During the reign of Edward VII, from 1901 to 1910, the Postmaster-General's annual reports show that a total of 5,920,933,334 postcards were sent in Britain; almost six billion. In one year alone, 1908, some 860 million postcards were sent. This means that, incredible as it may seem, almost two and a half million postcards were being posted every single day in 1908. It might not have been quite as popular as today's social media sites, but postcards really were tremendously popular at that time.

Fully to understand how picture postcards equated in many ways to the social media of today and the almost instantaneous exchange of messages which these media entail, it is necessary for us to know that there were in the towns and cities of Edwardian Britain at least six postal deliveries a day. It took only a few hours for a posted card to reach its destination in London and other large cities and the reply could be received as swiftly. It was perfectly possible for a person to despatch an enquiry in the morning, receive the reply at lunchtime and for the response to be in turn received by the late afternoon or early evening. Social arrangements were frequently made in this way, with somebody sending a card and inviting the recipient to meet him later that day. Confirmation would be with him before the evening and all without anybody needing to speak a word. It is this, the increasing use of written text to communicate with friends, which puts us strongly in mind of the present day and its social *mores*.

Today, there is a single postal delivery each day in Britain, which might take place at any time from early morning to late evening. A postcard or letter posted on one day may or may not arrive the next day; it would be unwise indeed to depend upon this being the case! This lamentable state of affairs is a relatively recent one. Sunday collections from pillar boxes ended in 2007. Until 2004, there were two postal deliveries a day, one early in the morning and the other at about lunchtime. The first post typically arrived before most people left for work in the morning. Until 1961, there were even deliveries on Christmas Day. This steady erosion of the postal service has meant that the one which we today enjoy is a pale shadow of that which once existed, with letters arriving regularly from six in the morning until ten at night.

The arrival of mass literacy at the end of the nineteenth century acted to spur on this explosion of written messaging. One could be reasonably confident by 1900 that whoever received a postcard would be able to read the message. In the early nineteenth century, it was not uncommon for those getting letters to have to find somebody who could read the thing out loud to them. For the first time in British history, working-class people were staying in touch on a regular basis by means of the written word.

The range and variety of picture postcards available to the Edwardians was staggering. They were not by any means restricted to the risqué seaside type of thing popularized by Donald McGill, although cards of that kind were certainly produced in vast numbers. Many were light-hearted and humorous, but every conceivable topic featured on picture postcards; politics, travel, motoring, sport, celebrities, relations between the sexes, to say nothing of cute animals. Images of kittens peeping out from a boot or a puppy on a roller-skate are often shared on social media and crop up on YouTube. The Edwardians were no different, kittens and puppies having the same attraction then as now. One artist whose works were very much in demand for postcards was Louis Wain, who specialized in cats who walked around on their hind legs and conducted themselves like humans.

Louis Wain's famous cats show another glimpse of life which will be familiar to the digital generation; the juxtapositioning of images and text to express a point more forcefully. Posts on Facebook and Twitter are often enlivened in this way, by pictures which bear a few words which emphasise and underline the message. The pictures of Louis Wain's cats were used in 'write away' cards, in which the message was already started off for the person sending the card. The caption, 'I was much surprised', printed in cursive handwriting beneath a picture of an expectant father cat being presented with a litter of kittens which had just been born is one example of this. Others might be, 'Sorry to keep you waiting' or 'Written in great haste', each accompanied by an appropriate picture.

Even simple pictures from a book could be used to convey or reinforce a message. Illustration 14 shows a scene from the once enormously popular humorous classic *Mrs Caudle's Curtain Lectures*. The caption reads, 'Mr Caudle, unable to stand Mrs Caudle's tongue any longer, goes to sleep with the children'. The postmark on this card shows that it was sent in 1905 and the message accompanying this image, seen in Illustration 15, is brief and to the point; 'Dear May, I wonder if this is how AJ goes on? Alf'. Obviously, the postcard was chosen as some kind of personal joke.

Much has been said in recent years of the way in which the use of emails and texts has resulted in a less formal and more relaxed mode of written communication. Abbreviations and slang are used, the old conventions of beginning written messages with 'Dear XXX' and ending with 'Yours faithfully' have all but vanished and many people do not even bother signing their names; knowing that the recipient will realize from whom the message comes. The same process took place during the period at which we have been looking, only with postcards, rather than texts.

Reading the messages on picture postcards sent in Edwardian Britain shows an amazing informality. One can hardly believe that the Victorians would have been so casual and sloppy in the language used in written communication! Often, there is no salutation at all and the writer just says at once what he wishes to convey. It is not uncommon for there to be no signing off either or perhaps just the initials of the person who sent the card. This is in part because many of these messages are very short; sometimes consisting of only half a dozen words; 'See you Wednesday', for example. There are distinct similarities here to posts on Twitter, where those writing are keenly aware that they must pare down to the bone what they wish to say. Fifty or sixty words is about the most that can be written on the back of a postcard. Just as in modern text messages, words are frequently omitted and others reduced to initials. For instance, we see sentences such as, 'Thanks for P.C.', which written in full would read, 'Thank you for the postcard'. Of course, some of this style of truncated language would be familiar to those who had sent telegrams, where one had to pay extra for a single word.

The abbreviated and slangy nature of many communications sent by postcard was a matter of great regret to older and more educated people in Edwardian Britain. Letter-writing had risen to the status of an art-form during the seventeenth and eighteenth centuries and now it was rapidly becoming a lost art; due entirely to the popularity of the picture postcard! Some volumes of collected letters had attained the status of classics; one thinks, for example, of Lord Chesterfield's *Letters to his Son and Others*. Novels too were written in epistolary form. Now, the English language was being debased and degraded and instead of elegant letters, people were just scrawling a few lines, with half the words reduced to one or two letters, along with many cryptic initials. Just as some people worry today about the ill effects of youngsters using text speak, so too were there concerns 110 years ago that people might eventually lose the ability to write in correct and coherent English.

The occasions on which postcards might be sent differed very greatly from what those of us who grew up in the late twentieth century might expect. By the time that the millennium arrived in 2000, the only time anybody might conceivably send a postcard would be while on holiday. The Edwardians though would be just as likely to send a postcard *to* somebody who was on holiday as they would be to send one when they were themselves on holiday. Just as we would think nothing of texting a friend while he was away for a week, so too would people in Edwardian Britain send a card to keep in touch with somebody they weren't likely to speak to in person for a while. This too resonates strongly with the present day.

It has been observed that some people today are seemingly unable to look at an interesting or memorable scene without reaching for their mobile phone and capturing the view electronically, usually to share with their friends. It was similarly remarked in the early 1900s that visitors to interesting places often spent more time choosing the best postcard on sale, one which showed the attraction to best advantage, than they did actually looking at the building or spectacular view itself. It was not just the British who suffered from this affliction. Jerome K. Jerome, best known as the author of *Three Men in a Boat*, was a regular traveller to Germany before the First World War. He wrote that the German tourist was so preoccupied with the buying and sending of postcards, that he didn't even know where he had been until he got home and looked at the postcards which he had sent to his family and friends!

Writing postcards became a constant activity for some people, just as today we see people texting all the time. It was not uncommon to see passengers on trains in Britain who spent the whole of the journey writing postcards. Many people carried a supply of postcards with them at all times. Postcards were even used to send greetings on people's birthdays and as Christmas cards. Today the convention with Christmas or birthday cards is that they are private greetings which we enclose in an envelope. It is common though to come across picture postcards sent during the period at which we are looking which bear only the words 'Happy Christmas' or 'Many Happy Returns of the Day'. Plainly, Christmas or birthday greetings were not in those days regarded as a strictly private matter between sender and recipient. Curiously, a relic of this distinction between private and public communication through the post lingered on in Britain until as late as 1968. Up until that year, a reduced rate was available for sending birthday and Christmas cards, but only on condition that the envelope was not sealed.

We have looked in this chapter at the growth of photography as a popular pastime and it was perhaps inevitable that this should become entangled with the craze for postcards. The desire of many people today to send photographs of themselves for others to see is nothing new. The Edwardian equivalent of the 'selfie' was the personalized postcard. In Chapter 9 we shall be looking at the concept of 'instant' cameras, those which produce a developed photograph in less than a minute. Such cameras were very popular with the Edwardians. Photographers used to ply their trade at fairs and beaches, providing visitors with souvenirs.

Cameras which took postcard-sized pictures were already on the market when the American company of Chicago Ferrotype came up with a brilliant new idea. Existing cameras which turned snapshots into postcards had to have the pictures developed in the ordinary way, that is in a darkroom, so that the finished product might not be seen for a few days. Obviously, these had their limitations. Day-trippers might not want to have their picture taken on the promenade if it meant waiting until they had returned home before they could even see the thing. What would be the point of having a picture postcard of yourself at the seaside a week after you'd got home? For this reason, postcard cameras were never really popular. The Chicago Ferrotype Company already produced cameras which turned out little photographs thirty seconds after the shutter clicked; what if one of these was made which could take postcard-sized pictures ready almost at once? In 1913, the Mandelette Postcard Camera was released and it was an enormous success.

The Mandelette was a fixed-focus camera, with a single shutter speed. It was very similar in appearance to the Box Brownie, being little more than a plain black cuboid. Unlike the Brownie though, the Mandelette featured an integral developing tank, into which the photographs dropped when they had been taken. This was a form of direct positive photography, in which the image appeared at once, without the need for negatives and so on. This process will be explained in Chapter 9. Perhaps the cleverest part of the whole thing was that the pictures were taken on cards which had already been printed on the back as postcards, with the spaces for message and address marked out. In other words, this camera meant that one could acquire a photograph of oneself and send it to a friend, knowing that it would arrive the same day that it had been taken.

There is something very modern about this idea, that within hours of a picture being taken, it will be seen by relatives and friends who might live miles away. The similarities to our own way of life are immediately apparent. Today, those on holiday will snap a picture and click 'send', knowing that the recipient will see it almost at once. For the Edwardian holidaymaker, the time lag between the click of the shutter might have been hours, rather than seconds, but the basic idea is precisely the same.

It was not only photographs which could be swiftly despatched with the guarantee that they would arrive within a matter of hours. Voicemail too made its appearance at about the same time. Telephones were not commonly found in domestic households, although they were becoming more common among the middle classes. Public telephones were beginning to be seen too; the first coin-operated callbox to appear in Britain was installed at Ludgate Circus Post Office in London in April 1906. Recorded messages, though, were delivered by quite another route.

In the late nineteenth century, there had been a 'format war' between the two main types of sound-recording apparatus; phonograph and gramophone. By the time that Edward VII became king though, this battle was all but over, with Thomas Edison's cylinders being routed by the discs of Berliner's gramophone. Gramophone records were far more practical for all kinds of applications than the wax cylinders of Edison's phonograph. For one thing, they could be miniaturized.

Very soon after inventing the phonograph, Edison proposed that it could be used in the future as a talking clock. Realistically, there was little prospect of phonograph cylinders being used for this purpose, but gramophone records were another matter entirely. In 1895 a watchmaker in Geneva called Mons Sivan put together the world's first talking watch. The pocket watch incorporated a tiny, hardened rubber disc which had forty-eight tracks inscribed upon it. These consisted of the twelve hours and thirty-six quarter-hours. Once wound, the watch would announce the time every fifteen minutes.

The fact that gramophone records could be made far smaller than the commercially-produced discs of music with which the Edwardians were familiar prompted a number of companies, both in Europe and America, to experiment with methods for sending pre-recorded messages which would reach the recipient in a few hours.

On 24 May 1905, a patent was applied for in Britain relating to:

A phonograph adapted to serve both as a recorder and a reproducer and which is especially intended for recording sounds upon phonogram cards prepared for the purpose and for reproducing the sounds recorded on said cards.

The expression 'phonogram cards' will perhaps need a little explanation. Phonograms, phonocards or phonopost (various other words were dreamt up to describe them), first appeared in 1903. The idea was simple enough, although the technical complications were great. A personal greeting was made on a small gramophone record, which was glued to a postcard. This was then popped in the post, to be played by the person to whom it was addressed. Put like that, it sounds straightforward enough and many companies in Britain, France, Germany and the United States were very keen to perfect the technology involved. If this could be done, then the phonogram card could become the next big thing in analogue communication technology. That was certainly how those working in the field viewed matters. On 17

November 1903, a German magazine devoted to gramophones and records, called *Phonographisch Zeitschrift,* carried an advertisement for what was claimed to be an 'epochal' invention. This was a recording and playback machine, very similar to that which would be patented in Britain eighteen months later. It was to revolutionize communications: this at least was the hope. After all, nobody would go to all the expense of buying two of these devices and a supply of blank discs just for the novelty value.

Those hoping to turn voicemails of this sort into a commercial success faced several difficulties. One was the material of which the recording should be made. Obviously, for a postcard which would be buffeted about during the sorting and delivery of mail, it would be no use if the material of which the record was made was either soft or brittle. The shellac used for ordinary gramophone records wouldn't do. Nor could they be too heavy. The hope was that the cards recorded in this way would weigh no more than ordinary postcards and would cost no more to send through the post. The whole aim was to ride on the back of the postcard craze and that could only be done if the cards could be sent as cheaply as any other postcard.

Emilien-Jean-Baptiste Brocherioux and Paul-Joseph Tochon made an application to the British Patent Office in 1905 for:

> The production of a special design to be applied to the surface of paper, cardboard, pasteboard and other substances to form a coating on which sounds may be recorded and subsequently reproduced by means of a phonograph. The invention is especially suitable for the production of phonogram cards.

Competition in being the first company to get this new method off the ground was intense. Three months after Emilen-Jean-Baptiste Brocherioux and Paul-Joseph Tochon had applied for their patents, the British Patent Office received another application from a man called Max Thomas, who was German. He had already filed patents in other European countries and now he wished to protect his invention in Britain. The Patent Application outlined his ideas:

> It has been proposed to enable persons, each provided with a gramophone, to converse with the other by sending through the post a postcard or letter composed of paper or celluloid which has been previously impressed by the recording device of the sender's instrument.

The patent went on to say that so light would these records be, that there would be no increase in postage; they would not cost more to send than an ordinary postcard or letter. On 17 March 1905, the *Daily Mirror* carried an article about Max Thomas, which told how he had been trying to market what were described as 'singing postcards' in Britain.

Many other inventors and companies became involved in what a lot of people saw as the next revolution in communications. It was a time of exciting innovation in analogue technology and some people claimed that talking postcards were destined in the future to be as significant as radio. It was not to be. Today, hardly anybody has even heard of the things and those who have, see them in their proper place as merely being a curious novelty. There were two reasons for this.

Perhaps the main thing holding back the widespread adoption of recordings sent by post was that it was necessary to have some kind of mechanical equipment to play the things, once they were received. It was hardly worth buying one of the specialized recording and playback units, unless you were sure that you would be sending and receiving a lot of these cards. There would, in the same way, only be any point in recording a message and sending it to an acquaintance if you were sure that he or she possessed one of the devices. Unless they became as commonly used in the average household as a gaslights or stoves, then why bother despatching such a communication?

Of course, some systems could be recorded at home and played on ordinary gramophones, but there was still the initial expense of purchasing a recording machine. Gramophones were not often to be found in the average home either. One company, Sonorine, hoped to find a way round the reluctance of consumers to risk buying a machine which might turn out to be a useless white elephant. In France, they set up coin-operated recording booths, where for a modest sum one could record a greeting which could be played back on any gramophone. The scheme was not a success and by 1914, it was obvious to everybody that the talking postcard was a technological dead-end. There were intermittent attempts to revive the idea and even as late as the 1950s, companies were still trying to market such things. By then, it was clear that exchanging messages in this way was really only a bit of fun. The gramophone in the home was only wanted for entertainment, which meant recorded music and singing.

We have seen that the Edwardian home was becoming a very different sort of place than it had been when Victoria was on the throne. At that time, the only homes containing printed matter and photographs would have been those of the well-to-do or at least the middle classes. The vast majority of people in Britain would have had no newspapers, magazines or books lying around. Nor would letters or photographs have been much in evidence in the average domestic setting. By 1910, all these things would have been extremely common in all but the poorest of households. There would be recently-received postcards propped up on the mantelpiece, perhaps the odd newspaper or popular magazine on the table, possibly even a few family photographs here and there. The Analogue Revolution was sweeping through the country and its manifestations were beginning to be seen and heard everywhere.

Photography and the reading of newspapers might no longer have been the exclusive preserve of the middle classes in Edwardian Britain, but other developments of analogue technology certainly were, although of course they too would eventually filter down to the homes of ordinary working men and women in a few decades. The gramophone was becoming increasingly popular and gradually, but inexorably, replacing the piano as a means of entertainment in the evening. It was an expensive pastime though; beyond the financial reach of most people. Although by 1903, over 100,000 different gramophone recordings were available, they were very expensive. Records at that time came in three different sizes; seven, ten and twelve inches in diameter. They varied dramatically in price. A seven-inch record of some relatively obscure musician might retail for only a shilling (5p). A twelve-inch record featuring a famous star such as Caruso though, might cost £1, twenty times as much! Even the cheaper records would be out of the financial reach of most people at a time that a manual worker might be earning just 7d (3p) an hour.

Those early gramophones, with their enormous brass horns, have become iconic, symbolizing the emerging technology in the run-up to the First World War. One may be seen in Illustration 16. Their days were numbered though. With the development of electronic amplifiers such as de Forest's triode valve in 1906, it was clear that the way forward with amplification of sound lay not with increasingly sophisticated horns, made of metal or wood, but rather with the use of electricity. Even without electrical recording or amplification, the horns on the old-style gramophones were beginning to look a little absurd, even to the Edwardians, leading in 1907 to the concealed horn and then, two years later, to the 'Pigmy Grand', the world's first hornless, and portable, gramophone.

The telephone too was becoming more common, especially in the years immediately before the start of the First World War, when its use increased exponentially. In 1902, the *Times* commented that the telephone was 'a convenience for the well-to-do and a trade appliance for persons who can very well afford to pay for it'. In other words, apart from prosperous businesses, only the wealthy could consider having a telephone in their home. It is worth reminding ourselves at this point that until 1975, the majority of British homes did not have telephones in them.

It was from 1911 that the use of the telephone really took off and became something to which the middle-class family, as well as the rich, could aspire. In that year, when the telephone system was taken over by the General Post Office, there were 663,000 telephones in the country. About a third of the domestic telephones at that time were in London, with the rest being also largely restricted to big cities. With the effective nationalisation of the telephone system, demand suddenly rocketed. In 1911, just over 42 million calls were made. Within two years, this figure grew ten-fold. In 1913, 486 million calls were made, almost half a billion.

Despite their wider use, both telephones and gramophones were rarely to be seen in the average home. A much cheaper technology though was finding its way into people's lives and not just those with plenty of money either. The 'crystal detector' or 'cat's whisker' radio was cheap and easy to build and experiment with. It needed no power source and practically anybody could construct and operate one. 'Detector' crystals of the lead ore, galena, began to be marketed with radio enthusiasts in mind and purpose-built components also appeared for sale. In America, a magazine called *Modern Electrics* began publication in April 1908. Originally, this was intended to put those who wished to conduct their own experiments in this field in touch which suppliers of radio parts, but as time passed it began to feature articles on how to build crystal radio sets and rig up aerials. That there was considerable amateur interest in radio is shown by the rapidly-rising circulation of *Modern Electrics*. In 1908, the circulation was 2,000; by 1911, this had risen to 52,000.

In Britain too, curious people were buying crystals of galena, rigging long aerials out of the windows and seeing if they could pick up any of the transmissions being made. Radios of this sort did not need batteries or any other external source of power, which made them cheap and easy to experiment with. If one stretched out a long wire, the longer the better, then any radio waves would induce in it a very slight current. This current would be carried to the receiver, where the listener would strain to try and hear something of interest through the headphones. Without amplifiers, any signals were very faint and complete silence was needed to hear them.

An amusing anecdote which illustrates perfectly the kind of thing which was happening in many British homes at this time, as ordinary people attempted to get to grips with the exciting new methods of communication, may be found in an account of childhood at that time. In a book called *Marjie – The True Story of an Edwardian Girl*, the story is told of how a young girl's father and brothers tried, before the First World War, to build a crystal radio:

> The boys and their father tried their hands at producing crystal radio sets and Horatio [the father] was very excited when he heard the unmistakeable sound of a barrel organ.
>
> He called the children to listen but was a little perplexed to find out that the sound was louder away from his radio set. It was the sharp-eyed Marjorie who first spotted the Barrel Organ Player, complete with monkey, entering their street.

So faint were the unamplified signals picked up by crystal detectors of this kind, that such situations must have been common.

One of the themes at which we have looked is the fact that information revolutions tend to have similar features, regardless of the nature of the technology which precipitates them. This may be seen particularly clearly in the case of the 'cat's whisker' type of radio receiver. One of the complaints of modern parents is that their offspring are often so wedded to new communication technology that they are unavailable for ordinary family life. They are either preoccupied with their mobile phones, playing computer games or busy on the Internet. Whatever the reason, they seem more interested in what is going on with some electronic gadget than they are with talking to their mothers and fathers!

Forty years ago, the teenage girl gossiping on the telephone with her friend, oblivious to the family around her, was a stock figure in cartoons. Fifty years ago, it was the teenager with a transistor radio held to his or her head which illustrated the belief that technology was alienating young people from real life. In earlier eras, television or cinema was to blame and before this 'Penny Dreadfuls', or even novels! Once the construction and use of crystal sets became a craze, the image of a boy with headphones clamped firmly over his ears and a look of intense concentration on his face, began to appear in magazines such as *Punch*. The captions to cartoons about this showed that the mothers were complaining that they were never able to talk to their children anymore, because they now spent all their spare time listening to what was going on in other parts of the world!

It is time now to look outside the home and consider some of the ways in which the analogue revolution was affecting society at large. We have touched upon some aspects of this already, but there are areas which we have not yet explored, where new information technology was causing a revolution in everyday life.

Chapter 7

How the Analogue Revolution
Changed Edwardian Society

The first fourteen years of the twentieth century saw the foundations of the modern world being laid in more than one way. The technology which came into general use at that time, not only in Britain but also across America and Europe, certainly revolutionized the way that people lived and how they communicated with each other. It was responsible also for deeper changes than the purely superficial ones of listening to the wireless or going to the cinema in the evenings instead of staying at home and playing the piano or reading, as the Victorians had done. Society itself was irrevocably altered by the tidal wave of information and data which engulfed it between 1901 and 1914. The very machinery of the Edwardian information revolution also triggered major social changes. Nowhere was this more evident than in Britain.

In Victorian Britain, ideas on the separate ways in which men and women should conduct themselves were very different from those to which we now subscribe. Equality of opportunity for men and women is now taken for granted and those who oppose such a view are regarded as dinosaurs. This perception is now so well established that it can be difficult for us to see how radically different were the prevailing views a little over a century ago.

In the Western World during the nineteenth century, the two sexes were thought to be suited to altogether different spheres, namely the public and private. A sharp distinction was drawn between these two arenas of action. On the one hand, men operated in public, in fields such as politics, law, medicine, science and the arts. For women, though, the natural place of work and the focus of their activity was the home. Caring for children, cooking, cleaning and mending clothes was their sphere of action. This was all thought to be tied in with a form of biological determinism. Men were, by their very physical and mental abilities, believed to be vigorous and commanding. Women, by contrast, were nurturing and submissive, lacking the strength and intellect which men inherited as a matter of course. Alfred,

Lord Tennyson, Poet Laureate for an astonishing forty-two years of Queen Victoria's reign, summed the matter up neatly in *The Princess*:

> Man for the field, woman for the hearth,
> Man for the sword, for the needle she:
> Man with the head and woman with the heart,
> Man to command and woman to obey.

This almost universal attitude in Victorian Britain meant that any respectable woman working outside the home ran the risk of being seen as suspect and laid herself open to the accusation of 'unsexing' herself. Even going out and about unaccompanied by a man meant that women could be viewed a little askance. A lone woman in a public house might easily be taken for a prostitute.

The two commonest and most acceptable ways for women to earn a living were both in private homes. For working-class girls, being 'in service' was a way of leaving their parental homes without quitting the domestic sphere. Middle-class women, on the other hand, could become governesses. Florence Nightingale helped to breach this convention with her example in the Crimean War, but she was very much an exception. It was not until the late nineteenth and early twentieth centuries that careers outside the home, suitable for well brought-up and educated young women, began to appear. Factories and shops might provide some limited opportunities for working-class women, but for those wishing to abide by convention, there was little, other than the exceptions mentioned above.

Things were very different for boys and men, whatever their social class. It was expected as a matter of course that they would take part in the world and make their mark in some way. In manual trades, there was of course a tradition of young boys being apprenticed to craftsmen and then learning the trade and progressing until they became blacksmiths, coopers, carpenters or builders themselves. For lower middle-class boys, there was a similar system for clerical work, particularly in the Civil Service. So-called 'boy copyists' were employed for a much lower wage than an adult earned and their job was to copy letters and documents by hand. Without typewriters, carbon paper and copiers, copying written material by hand was a big part of the work in an office. As they grew older, these boys would hope to obtain more important posts in the government department or counting house in which they worked. The problem with boys is that they tend to be troublesome and unreliable and those engaged for their ability to write legibly in copperplate handwriting were as quarrelsome and prone to mischief as their contemporaries who were being trained as artisans.

Towards the end of the nineteenth century, the typewriter began to replace the pen in many larger businesses. A competent typist, or 'type-writing operative' as they were known in those days, could produce text at two or three times the speed of somebody writing by hand. What's more, carbon paper meant that another couple of copies of what was being typed could be produced at the same time as the original. As the typewriter found its way into commercial offices and government departments, young women came with them.

There were two problems about using boys for routine clerical tasks such as copying. One was that they did not remain boys for very long and as they grew older they wanted more responsible positions and higher wages. It was then necessary to go to all the trouble of training another boy, who would in turn, after a few years, be leaving. In addition to the high turnover and constant need to train new workers, there was also the indisputable fact that a department full of boys tended to be a noisy and wild place, somewhere which needed strict and constant supervision. A room full of young women aged between 18 and 30 would, on the other hand, be a different proposition entirely. They would be quieter, more mature, easier to control and with no ambition of furthering themselves by applying for an office job with more responsibility, the Civil Service in those days being an exclusively masculine establishment. These women might remain not just for a year or two, but could be trained and then carry on with their job, becoming better and better at it as the years passed, for a decade or more. Illustration 17 shows such a typewriter operative at work.

Perhaps because women were thought to be deft with their fingers through needlework and embroidery, it was from the beginning assumed that women would be better able to operate typewriters than men. So it was that 'boy copyists' began to be edged out of offices and replaced by young women typists. A similar process had taken place with the telephone exchanges which were becoming larger and more widespread. Boys were cheeky and unreliable, and many users reported that they preferred to hear women's voices anyway when ringing to be put through to a number.

The burgeoning technology of Edwardian Britain thus provided job opportunities for well-brought-up young women. In a sense, these typists and telephonists were the vanguard of women entering the workplace. Once the principle was firmly established that respectable girls could work outside the domestic sphere in this way, it acted to normalise the idea and make people accept the sight of a young woman in an office. It was the beginning of women being regarded as just a natural and unremarkable part of the working world. Illustration 18 shows a telephone exchange staffed entirely by women. This was a respectable, white-collar job that any daughter of a clergyman or doctor could take without any loss of status or suggestion that she was behaving in an unwomanly fashion.

Of course, these new job opportunities for women came along at roughly the same time that the movement for female emancipation emerged as a major force in British politics. Because the suffragists and then suffragettes became newsworthy just when cheap, illustrated newspapers and cinema were becoming a major influence, it was hardly possible to ignore their activities and slogans. The very name of the most militant faction among the suffragists, those who were later known as 'suffragettes', was coined by the *Daily Mail*. Emily Davison's death beneath the hooves of the King's racehorse was filmed by the Pathé company and thus seen by millions of people across the country as the resulting film was screened not only in cinemas, but also at the end of the music hall variety shows which were so enormously popular at that time.

The suffragette struggle, widely reported in the new mass media, combined with the new openings for young women to work outside the home, acted in synergy to alter the perspective of women which had been the prevailing doctrine for centuries. Without the technological innovations at which we have looked in this book, it is highly unlikely that the status of women in society would have changed so radically in such a short space of time.

The inequality between men and women was only one aspect of Victorian Britain which had been festering for years and now threatened to come to a head. There were other fundamental problems in society as it was constituted at the end of the nineteenth century and these caused from time to time fierce discontent, which periodically erupted in violence. Rioting, fighting with the police after the public houses had closed and muggings were routine occurrences in nineteenth-century Britain. Sometimes, there were organized protests, such as those of the Chartists in the early years of Victoria's reign, but in the general way of things riots were spontaneous and largely chaotic actions triggered by strictly local grievances. It could hardly be otherwise.

Those who were living on the edge of poverty in one provincial town had little way of knowing if their situation was shared by many others throughout the country. For all they knew, they were simply unlucky and everywhere else in Britain working men and women were thriving. Similarly, although factory workers in, say, the north of England might be aware that the owner of the factory enjoyed a higher standard of living than the factory hands, that was about all that they did know. They did not come into contact with rich people, nor have any idea how such people lived or of the type and amount of food which the wealthier members of society consumed. Not only did they not know such things, even if they had, the knowledge would not have been much use to them. Most were illiterate and even those who were not had no readily available means of communicating with friends or relatives living elsewhere in the country. They had no spare money to buy paper and envelopes to write letters and even if they had done, a penny for a stamp could mean the difference between buying a loaf of bread or going hungry.

Rebellion against the established order then tended to be sometimes violent, but always local. A rash of strikes might afflict a city or district, but these were easily suppressed by calling out the military, a regular event at that time. Without access to reliable information about politics and the debates in Parliament, there was no real possibility of any growth of political awareness among the masses of ordinary men and women. There was therefore no sense of wider interest in the political landscape or any realisation that alternative methods of ordering society existed.

Everything changed politically and socially with the coming of the mass media in the years following the death of Queen Victoria in 1901. The change did not of course take place overnight, following the Queen's death on 22 January that year, but differences began to be noticeable within a year or two. These were wholly unconnected with the death of a monarch, but related rather to those inventions, and refinements of existing inventions, at which we have been looking in previous chapters.

Newspapers carried a great deal of information, allowing an Edwardian factory worker to be infinitely more conscious of what was happening in his own country that had been the case even a decade earlier. The *Daily Mail* began publication for a halfpenny in 1896 and of course the tabloid *Daily Mirror* was circulating less than a decade later. These newspapers allowed people to keep up to date with events both in Britain and overseas. Some papers supported the Liberal party and others the Conservatives. In 1912, the *Daily Herald* appeared; which was left-wing and called for radical social change. Simply knowing about what was happening throughout the country was a novel experience for the average worker at that time.

We have seen that the films shown at music halls were sometimes so-called 'topicals', the forerunner of news and current affairs programmes. The Pathé newsreel became a way to see what was happening in the rest of the country and even the wider world. Films of strikers clashing with police in London and Liverpool would let a working man know that his struggle against capitalism was not a purely local affair and that other men, in a similar position to him, were also fighting to improve their condition. By watching newsreels and reading the popular press, ordinary people learned something about the political affairs which affected them.

What the Edwardian period saw was growth in political consciousness of the working class. It was a process fuelled by advances in information technology. The Linotype and Monotype machines, the halftone photographs which appeared in those newspapers and also the moving pictures which were becoming a regular part of their hours of leisure, all combined to ensure that workers increasingly understood that the way the world was organized today might not be an accurate predictor of how it would be in a year or two's time. The monotonous cycle of switching between Whigs and Tories, Liberals and Conservatives, had been running for centuries. For most British citizens, it made not the least difference to their lives which of the two great political parties held office; things would not change for them and they accordingly took little interest in politics. Charles Dickens satirised this recurring and, for most people, pointless and irrelevant turn-taking of the great political parties in *Bleak House*. He describes how Boodle, Coodle and Doodle on the one hand are succeeded by Buffy, Cuffy and Duffy, without anybody noticing any real change in the social system.

As the first decade of the twentieth century drew on, however, and the great mass of the population grew to be more aware of what was going on, a new spirit began to emerge. Instead of seeing themselves as and their lives as being a purely local struggle, some men and women began to realize that they and their class had much in common, whether they lived in Scotland or England, Glasgow or London, Manchester or Leeds. Through reading about and seeing what was going on in Britain and also America and Russia, working-class people understood that things might change and that there were other ways of running a country, besides voting for the Liberals or Conservatives.

In practical terms, this dawning class consciousness was manifested in the rapid growth of the Labour Party. In 1900, somewhere in the region of 62,000 people voted Labour in the general election and this led to two MPs entering Parliament for the party. Six years later, five times as many people voted Labour and thirty MPs entered the House. By 1910, there were forty-two Labour MPs and the slow decline of the Liberal Party was about to begin. Of course, this was not solely due to the influence of cheap newspapers and the Pathé newsreels! Many other factors were at work. However, it was the new awareness of the unfairness of the system into which they had been born which was promoted by the reading of newspapers and watching of newsreels about current affairs.

The rise of the Labour Party in Britain was made easier by another innovation in information and communication technology, one that is seldom heard of today. At one time, copying machines were the cheapest and most straightforward way of printing circulars, newsletters and pamphlets. With the advent of computers and printers, however, they have gone the same way as carbon paper and typewriter ribbons.

Using movable type to set out a page and then print it, the method used for turning out printed matter since the days of Caxton and Gutenberg, was still the commonest way of printing ephemera in the late nineteenth century. By 1900 though, new methods were becoming popular, stencils which could be fitted on a drum and used to reproduce typed lettering.

The mimeograph was cheap, simple, robust and easy to use. Indeed, mimeographs were still being used as late as the 1970s to make copies of school newsletters, fan magazines and so on. The process was simple, although there were many minor variations. The first step was to prepare a stencil. A sheet of waxed paper was inserted into an ordinary typewriter. The ribbon was removed, so that the sharp metal letters struck the waxed surface of the paper directly. This had the effect of removing the wax from the area hit by the letter, leaving a clear impression in the wax. The paper was only waxed on one side and was made of a peculiarly fibrous material, such as would allow ink to be absorbed and passed readily from one side of the paper to the other.

Once the stencil was ready, it was fastened to a roller which was saturated with ink. This was then rotated against a flat bed, where a sheet of paper was laid. The pressure forced ink from the roller and squeezed it through the parts of the paper which were no longer cover in wax, i.e. the printed letters.

The quality of mimeographed documents was nowhere near as good as those printed in the traditional way and the stencils wore out after a few hundred copies, but this was a fast and cheap means of preparing pamphlets and so on. As such, it was ideally suited to struggling political groups, such as the Labour Party in the early years of the twentieth century, which might not have the money to spare to pay for professionally-printed matter.

There was another great advantage of mimeograph machines when it came to political posters, handbills and circulars. There was a legal duty that such propaganda should bear both the printer's name and the name and address of the publisher. This was so that those who wished to incite their followers to violence or sedition could be brought to book. Some printers were a little wary of working with political groups who were too radical or outrageous in their views. They were right to be cautious, because the risk of prosecution run by printers whose clients advocated extremist views was a very real one. It was necessary only to look at the case of Sidney Drew, manager in 1914 of the London-based Victory House Printing House Company. Drew's company printed the newspaper of the Women's Social and Political Union (WSPU), the members of whom were commonly known as suffragettes. As sometimes happens with derogatory nicknames, the WSPU had enthusiastically adopted for themselves the term 'suffragette' and even called the newspaper which they published *The Suffragette*. Some of the articles which appeared in *The Suffragette* overstepped the boundary of acceptable political comment, however, and in the early summer of 1914, Sidney Drew, who was ultimately responsible legally for the contents of the paper, received a summons to appear in July at the Central Criminal Court in London; more commonly known as the Old Bailey. It is impossible to say whether the manager of the Victory House Printing Company fully realized the peril in which he found himself. The summons suggested that he was personally liable for the 2 January 1914 issue of *The Suffragette*, which meant that he was charged with:

> Soliciting, inciting and endeavouring to persuade divers women, members of the Women's Social and Political Union, and others to commit malicious damage to property.

Had he paid a little more attention to what he and his company were printing, then it is possible that Sidney Drew might have noticed that *The Suffragette* was urging women to break windows and carry out other acts of vandalism. If so, then he really should have been a little more careful about what he was helping to distribute. When he appeared at the Old Bailey in July 1914, Drew was convicted and sent to prison for two months.

Most printers were more scrupulous than Sidney Drew in the kind of thing which they helped publish and most tended to err on the side of caution. For this reason, left-wing activists in Edwardian Britain often found difficulty in getting printers to take their business. Even printing an appeal for workers to come out on strike could put them in a dangerous position legally and few wished to take chances. It is for this reason that the mimeograph was such a godsend for the fast-growing Labour Party. Questionable material could be prepared and printed by a typewriter to make the stencils and a relatively cheap mimeograph machine to print them. Such machines, which included the Cyclostyle manufactured by the German Gestetner company, had the effect of making printing available to the masses. As was remarked above, this was the first time in history that almost every adult person in Britain was able to read, which meant that any leaflet handed out would be pretty sure to be read by at least a few people.

The world of 1914 was very different from that of 1901, the year that Queen Victoria died. Many of the changes seen in Britain over the course of those few years were a consequence, some direct and others not, of the coming of the mass media. This in turn was a result of innovations in the field of information and communications technology. In this way, things like the Linotype machine and halftone photograph ultimately played a role in events ranging from the rise of the Labour Party to the outbreak of war in 1914 and the enfranchisement of women.

Chapter 8

Two Architects of the Analogue Revolution

W e are all of us familiar with such household names as Marconi and Thomas Edison, whom we understand to have been the fathers of, respectively, the radio and the first sound-recording apparatus. Although these were the men who reaped the rewards and fame for their work in analogue information and communication technology, Marconi even winning a Nobel Prize for his contribution to the development of radio, they were by no means the only or even the most important inventors working in the field at that time. History comprises a process of selection, highlighting some people and events while discarding others. Because of this winnowing out, although the name of Thomas Alva Edison is known to all educated men and women, that of Valdemar Poulsen is not. Neither is that of the man who was responsible above all others for starting the electronic revolution of the twentieth century, which gave birth to radio, television, radar, long distance telephony and many other things. This was Lee de Forest, who invented, among other things, the triode valve, for more than half a century an integral part of every radio.

We begin by looking at the life and career of the man sometimes referred to as the 'Danish Edison'. Valdemar Poulsen was born in Copenhagen in 1869. He came from a comfortably-off family background. His father was a judge. Despite the fact that young Valdemar's interest was almost entirely in physics, his father wanted him to be a doctor. So it was that after leaving school, Poulsen studied medicine at Copenhagen University. After devoting four years to this pursuit, which did not in the least appeal to him, he gave up university and in 1893 got a job as a technician with the Copenhagen Telephone Company, a terrible step down socially for a young man from such a respectable family!

It was while working for the telephone company that Poulsen came up with an idea which was to have such an influence on the world; that of magnetic recording. At the time, the only methods for recording sound were the relatively crude phonographs and gramophones which relied upon the mechanical engraving of wiggly grooves in tinfoil, wax or shellac. How, thought the Danish telephone technician, if the human voice could be converted into electrical impulses and these then used to magnetize a piece of wire. Surely, it would then be possible to decode these magnetized sections and recreate the sound which had created them?

The first experiment which Poulsen carried out could hardly have been simpler and it is, in retrospect, astonishing that nobody had thought of conducting such a test before. He stretched a length of steel piano wire from one end of a room to another, sloping down at a gentle angle. An electromagnet was attached to this wire in such a way that it could slide slowly from top to bottom. To this electromagnet, a battery-powered microphone was connected, into which somebody spoke while the electromagnet was travelling along the wire. When Poulsen then brought the electromagnet back to the top of the wire and replaced the microphone with a telephone earpiece, he was highly gratified to find that it was possible to play back the original speech. He had, by carrying out an absurdly simple procedure, demonstrated the principle of, among other things, the tape recorder and the computer hard drive.

In 1898, Poulsen patented his invention, calling it the telegraphone, but it proved difficult to find financial backers prepared to hazard their capital to exploit it. He was simply too far in advance of his time; nobody could really see the point of such a thing. It was an intriguing novelty, to be sure, but what *use* was it? The prototype of the magnetic recorder which Poulsen patented used the same steel wire as in his early tests. This was wound around a cylinder or drum and the recording head moved along the wire, just as in the initial experiments. It took a little while for him to realize that moving the electromagnet along the wire was not the easiest or most efficient method for his recorder and that it would make far more sense to draw the wire past the recording head, the technique used by all subsequent machines of this sort.

In 1900 the telegraphone was exhibited at the World Exposition in Paris, where it was most successful. Members of the public could record their voices and then listen to them being played back. One of those who spoke into the machine and was enchanted to hear his own voice for the first time was Franz Joseph, the Emperor of Austria. Franz Joseph's voice is the earliest magnetic recording in existence and may be heard on YouTube. Poulsen won a Grand Prix for the telegraphone, but was still unable to find backers who would help put the thing into production.

There were two chief disadvantages to the telegraphone as Poulsen presented it in Paris in 1900. One was that the running time was limited to just thirty seconds, confirming its status as little more than a parlour toy.

The second, and more serious, was that there was no way of amplifying the sound. There was no loudspeaker and one needed to strain even to hear a voice clearly through the telephone earpiece which was used. This problem also afflicted early radios as well and was to be solved by another pioneer of electronics, at whom we shall look later in this chapter.

There can be no doubt that Valdemar Poulsen was a man of great vision and reading his patents is like seeing into the future of communications and data storage throughout the twentieth century. He foresaw much that was to come, even if the scientific progress in the opening years of the century was not sufficiently advanced for him to put all his ideas into practice. Consider this passage from one of Poulsen's patents at that time, in which he speculates freely about other ways in which his telegraphone might be developed and talks of:

> . . . as a receiving device a steel band, supported if necessary on an insulating material and brought under the action of an electromagnet. Such an arrangement has the advantage that a steel band of a desired length may be used. Instead of a cylinder there may be used a disk of magnetizable material over which the electromagnet may be conducted spirally; or a sheet or strip of some insulating material such as paper may be covered with a magnetizable metallic dust and may be used as the magnetizable surface. With the aid of such a strip which may be folded, a message received at any place provided with the new apparatus may be sent to another place where it may be repeated by passing the strip through the apparatus at that place.

In short, as early as 1902 Poulsen had laid the groundwork for tape recorders, magnetic strips on bank cards, floppy discs, hard drives and much else besides.

A backer was finally found for the telegraphone in America, where the American Telegraphone Company was established in Springfield, Massachusetts. By 1903, they were promoting the telegraphone as an office dictation machine and also the world's first automatic telephone answering machine. This really was way ahead of its time and there was only very limited demand for such a gadget in the average office. One was installed by the Royal Dockyards in Britain, but for most offices, missed telephone calls out of hours were not a serious-enough problem to warrant such an expense as an answering machine.

The telegraphone might have been an invention for which the world was not yet ready, but the same could not be said by another project upon which Valdemar Poulsen worked. This was the arc converter, sometimes known as the Poulsen arc. It will be recalled from an earlier chapter that sending music or speech on radio waves, as opposed to simply transmitting the dots and dashes of Morse code, was all but impossible when working with apparatus which generated individual sparks. Poulsen worked on, and eventually found a way of using in radio transmissions, a spark-gap generator which produced an arc.

An electric arc is the process whereby the electrical decomposition or breakdown of a gas results in a continuous electrical discharge. The ordinary energy-saving electric light bulbs in our homes are an example of electric arcing. A current flows through them, between two terminals separated only by a gaseous mixture. Poulsen's genius lay in experimenting until he came up with an arrangement which caused an electric arc to generate electromagnetic waves which could be used in radio communications. He found that by using a carbon cathode and a copper anode, with hydrogen gas separating them, radio waves ranging between a few kilohertz and tens of kilohertz were produced. These continuous waves could be modulated and so used to carry vastly more information than that sent by mere sparks.

Poulsen patented the arc converter in 1903 and for the next twenty years, until the advent of vacuum tube transmitters, it was really the only method for sending continuous, sinusoidal waves of the kind necessary to transmit sound by radio. Valdemar Poulsen can, with some justification, be cited along with Marconi as the founding father of radio. The second inventor at whom we shall look in this chapter has also been called the 'father of radio'. His contribution to the field was slightly different, although no less important, to that made by Poulsen. Together, these two men made radio broadcasts possible and turned radio into the third of the mass media which dominated the twentieth century.

Lee de Forest's work in radio affected not only that medium, but also gramophones, telephones and cinema. Fully to understand the significance of his work, a brief diversion will be needed into the difficulties experienced by those hoping to manufacture gramophones which would be as satisfying to listen to as the original performances which they had recorded. The relevance of this to the other inventions mentioned above will become apparent as we explore the sound reproduction of early phonographs and gramophones.

One of the great difficulties in such early devices as Poulsen's telegraphone was that weak signals could not be multiplied or amplified. This was a great stumbling block to the development of everything from gramophones and talking movies to domestic radio sets. Various ideas were tried to increase the sound from an earphone or gramophone horn, but none was successful until an American inventor called Lee de Forest became involved.

Early efforts to amplify the sound from gramophones depended upon purely physical effects. In 1900 and for some years afterwards, the sound from the needle running along the groove of the record was increased by creating a kind of echo chamber. The sound travelled from the needle, along a hollow metal arm and then to a sound-box, finally emerging from a large horn. Such a contraption may be seen in Illustration 16. The picture is from a postcard advertising Beecham's Pills. This references the atrocious sound of early records and cylinders, because the little child is pouring a handful of Beecham's Pills into the horn of the phonograph, saying 'Sounds as if he wants some'. The tone of these early gramophones and phonographs was tinny and not wholly pleasing to those who enjoyed music. Gramophone horns were generally made of metal and it was found that a more mellow tone could be produces by making them of laminated wood, but this still could not actually magnify the sound. This difficulty was solved mechanically in a most ingenious, if ultimately unsatisfactory, fashion.

The idea of using compressed air to amplify a weak sound enjoyed something of a vogue in the years leading up to 1914. The idea behind compressed–air gramophones was very simple. An electric motor drew in and compressed a stream of air, which was then released through a valve and into the usual horn of gramophones of this time. The valve itself was of curious construction, consisting of two flat metal combs, which almost overlapped each other, but gave just enough room for the flow of compressed air to pass between them. One of these combs was connected to the tone arm of the gramophone and when a record was played, the comb vibrated, sometimes allowing more and at other times less compressed air to pass through the space between the two combs. This modulated flow of air reproduced the sound passing from the stylus of the gramophone.

Compressed–air gramophones proved very effective, some would say too effective. There was no possibility of adjusting the volume and so they were not altogether suitable for domestic use. In theatres, there were stories of those sitting in the front row getting up and moving to the back, because the sound was painfully loud. Sitting close to a compressed–air loudspeaker would have been like being near a factory hooter or a klaxon. Public-address systems using compressed air were tried out in both the Blackpool Tower and the Eiffel Tower in Paris. It was said that the one operating from the top of the Eiffel Tower was clearly audible across the whole of Paris. Something a little gentler and more easily controlled was needed for the amplification of radios and gramophones that compressed air. In 1906, it arrived and, along with the diode or vacuum valve which had been invented the previous year, ushered in the age of electronics.

Before going any further, it might be helpful to remind readers what is actually meant by the word 'electronics', a term which is bandied about freely today, without many people troubling to consider what they really saying when they talk of an electronic device, for example.

A lot of the time in everyday life, we control a flow of electricity by purely mechanical means. Switching a light on in our home, for instance, just connects two pieces of metal and allows a current to flow through them from the mains to the light bulb. Plugging a hairdryer into a socket and switching it on is another example of the mechanical control of electricity. These are electrical or electro-mechanical devices. If we use electricity itself to control the flow of current, then that is electronic. It was electronics which allowed things such as gramophones, telephones, tape recorders, television and radio to become widely used and no longer merely curiosities. The man responsible for this was Lee de Forest and his work connected in many ways with Valdemar Poulsen's. Between them, it is no exaggeration to say that they helped to create the modern world.

In 1905, a British electrical engineer called John Ambrose Fleming came up with the idea of the diode, although it was to be many years before anybody called it that. Fleming invented the electrical equivalent of a one-way valve, which would allow current to flow in one direction but not the other. This was done by making a sealed glass bulb from which the air had been evacuated and arranging for a stream of electrons to be emitted by heating a filament or wire. These were attracted by the plate in the bulb and a current was therefore passed through the vacuum from filament to plate. This simple device proved crucial in the commercial exploitation of radio, among other things.

Lee de Forest saw that the Fleming valve could be altered slightly and used to amplify signals. By adding a fine grid between the two terminals in the valve and connecting this to a current, de Forest discovered that a very feeble signal sent along the terminal to the grid would have the effect of allowing a far greater current to flow through the triode, as the new type of valve was called. Electricity was therefore being used to control the flow of electricity and together, Fleming's diode and de Forest's triode ushered in the age of electronics.

Lee de Forest was born in the United States in 1873. His father was a church minister, who hoped that his son would follow in his footsteps and become a clergyman. The young de Forest though had other ideas and wished to study electrical engineering and physics, which he did at Yale. At one point, he was expelled, because his experiments in electricity had a disconcerting habit of fusing all the lights and when he did this on the occasion of a lecture by a visiting professor, the university had enough and threw him out. He later returned though to undertake a PhD. The subject of his dissertation was; 'Reflections of Hertzian Waves from the Ends of Parallel Wires'.

De Forest was utterly convinced that radio telephony had a great future. When he left Yale in 1899, radio transmissions consisted of only dots and dashes of Morse code. The dream was that one day articulate speech or even music might be carried on radio waves, but it was hard to see at that time how this might be achieved. There were two main obstacles, both of which were ultimately tackled by de Forest. One of these was that at the end of the nineteenth century, radio waves were generated by sparks leaping across gaps between terminals. This causes a sudden burst of radio waves, far too brief to carry any information beyond a simple dot or dash. The other problem was that these early transmissions were exceedingly feeble. Listening through an earpiece, one had to strain to distinguish the dots and dashes from the background noise and static. What was needed was some way of amplifying these weak signals.

After leaving university, de Forest applied for a job with both Marconi and Nikola Tesla. Neither was interested in employing the young man and so he took a fairly lowly position for a while with the Western Electric Company in Chicago. There, he worked on various ideas relating to radio, before deciding to strike out on his own. After several false starts, in 1902 he found a financial backer called Abraham White. What de Forest did not realize until it was too late was that White was a crook, who was more interested in inflating stock prices and manipulating financial markets than he was in bringing the benefits of radio to the world.

The company that Lee de Forest and Abraham White set up was called the American De Forest Wireless Telegraph Company and its avowed aim was the development of 'world-wide wireless', sometimes abbreviated to 'WWW'. There were some early and exciting achievements for the business, before things began to go wrong. As part of their claim to be promoting 'world-wide wireless', the company set up two radio stations in China and during the build-up to the Russo-Japanese war of 1905 were able to provide the London *Times* with up-to-the-minute information about the crisis.

Radiotelegraph stations were also constructed for the US Navy in Florida and Guantanamo Bay in Cuba.

During his time with the American De Forest Wireless Telegraph Company, Lee de Forest made what would be his greatest contribution to the field of electronics, the world's first electronic component. It is worth looking in detail at what this entailed, as for almost the whole of the twentieth century the amplifiers which he devised were an integral part of most radios and telephone systems.

Fully to understand the significance of de Forest's contribution to the worldwide success of radio, television and long-distance telephones, it will be necessary to look in detail at his most important contribution to the field of electronics, of which he may justly be said to be the founding father. This is the triode, which ushered in both the possibility of amplifying signals while at the same time making the transmission of radio waves far easier.

The accusation was later levelled at de Forest that his triode was only a variation of John Fleming's valve, which had been patented a few years before de Forest produced his triode. The Fleming valve, which became known in later years as the diode, simply prevented electricity flowing both ways through an electric circuit. It is for this reason that it was called a valve originally; it served the same function as a valve in a pipe of water, restricting and directing the direction of the flow.

Diodes are still used today in all electronic devices. For one thing, the current used when we plug something into the domestic mains supply is AC or Alternating Current. This means that it surges back and forth, changing direction many times each second. It is sent to homes in this way because AC can be transmitted further and more effectively than DC or Direct Current. It is however DC current which is needed for televisions, computers and everything else which we plug into the mains. We need to 'rectify' the current, which is to say convert it from AC to DC. For this, diodes are needed.

The big problem with reproducing sound in the early part of the twentieth century was that it was impossible to magnify or amplify the faint sounds produced by radios, gramophones and telephones. With radio, this was a very serious difficulty, one which prevented radio being used as a mass medium. It could not be a shared activity, because the faint feeble sound could really only be heard through earpieces. This didn't matter for a radio operator in a ship at sea; such a man didn't care what he looked like. For families at home though, it was another matter. A few years ago, electronics manufacturers were trying to promote the idea of 3D televisions. The drawback was that viewers would have to wear silly glasses while watching television. This was a deal breaker: people don't wish to look ridiculous while they are relaxing in the evening. Much the same thing happened with early radio sets. Families all had to put on earphones and cluster round the radio set, which was inconvenient and made them feel foolish. What they wanted was a loudspeaker, so that listeners could hear the programme and also chat among themselves when they felt like it.

The answer to the vexing problem of amplification was simple, once de Forest had put together his triode. The weak radio signal was fed into one terminal of the triode, where it would cause the current flowing through the valve to be increased. This slightly magnified signal would then be fed into another triode. Three triodes linked up in this way were called a 'cascade' and the result was that even the feeblest broadcasts could be rendered plainly audible, without the use of headphones.

Not only could triodes be used to amplify incoming signals, they could also be used to magnify outgoing transmissions as well, by means of feedback. De Forest thus made it possible for loudspeakers and effective transmitters to be built. Until the invention of the transistor, all radios and televisions would contain glass triodes of the kind first made by Lee de Forest. Older readers might recall how radios and televisions in the 1950s and 1960s might suddenly stop working. Most often, it was a valve which needed to be replaced.

In addition to his original work, Lee de Forest also improved upon the inventions of others. He did this with some of the machines which Valdemar Poulsen had put together. In 1913, de Forest got hold of one of Poulsen's telegraphone recording machines. These had been marketed in America for several years, although they had never really taken off. For most purchasers, it was clear that these were novelty items, rather than practical machines for the office. The recorded sounds were very tinny and often all but inaudible. De Forest wanted one of the wire recorders for a special purpose; he was hoping to put together a practical method for making talkies. The existing methods, using gramophones, were none of them really satisfactory. By using Poulsen's telegraphone and combining it with a cascade arrangement of his triode vacuum tubes, de Forest thought that he might be able to produce a sound loud enough to fill an auditorium. The idea was not a success, but it spurred de Forest on to find another and better way of introducing sound to movies; one which we use to this very day.

There had been efforts as early as 1907 to put a soundtrack directly onto a film at the same time that the subject was being filmed. This was get rid of the complicated systems used at that time to synchronize separate recordings with the film being shown. After failing with his attempts to use a Telegraphone to add sound to movies, de Forest came up with the method which we use to this day. The result was marketed as the Phonofilm system and it was indistinguishable from that used ever since.

Phonofilm might have been more technically advanced than the gramophones linked to pulleys which were then being used to coordinate sound and film, the method used in *The Jazz Singer,* but the quality of the sound was not as good. The gramophone records were clearer and louder than Phonofilm and the spoken word more distinct. It might have been a technical triumph, but it was nonetheless a commercial failure. It showed, however, that recording sound on the film itself, rather than separately, was the only sensible route to take, if talking pictures were to become a reality.

We have glanced in this chapter at the work of two engineers and inventors of whom hardly anybody today has heard. We have seen too, the roots of many of the things which we take for granted, such as the electronic amplification of sound and the storage of data on magnetized discs. It is no exaggeration to say that men like Valdemar Poulsen and Lee de Forest laid the foundations for information storage and long-distance communications throughout almost the whole of the twentieth century. Certainly, improvements were made and new devices introduced, but really, there was little change in the technology used to make telephone calls, take photographs or record sound until the dawn of our own age, that of digital communications. It is at the astounding durability of Edwardian technology that we shall look next, both in the sense of the principles underlying the telephones and radios but also in the resilience and robustness of the actual apparatus used.

Chapter 9

The Roots of Modern Technology

We have so far looked at the information and communication technology which developed during the Edwardian period and came to dominate the rest of the twentieth century, the mechanical and electro-mechanical devices which proved so durable and long-lasting that, a century later, many are still in perfect working order. For most of us though, these once-handy devices, the manual typewriters and clockwork gramophones, are no more than historical curiosities. It is interesting to read of them, but this is essentially the technology of the past, with no conceivable relevance to the modern world of cable television and digital telephones. In fact, most of the gadgets upon which we depend today, even the Internet itself, actually had their roots in this era. Whether we are using fibre-optic cables, computer hard drives or listening to digital music, the Edwardians had already established the principles behind these things and produced crude prototypes.

The Digital Revolution which engulfed the developed nations of the world in the late twentieth and early twenty-first centuries did not come from nowhere. The devices upon which it sometimes seems that we now depend have almost all existed in one form or another for many decades.

Perhaps more importantly, the psychological basis for the modern world was set out by the Edwardians. This has had a powerful effect in shaping our hopes and expectations of what the world should look like. Most of the features of our own information revolution, the Digital Revolution, were predicted or at least envisaged over a century ago. Even as people in the early twentieth century were slowly coming to terms with such novelties as aeroplanes and radio, there were those who could see much farther into the future and had already mapped out in some ways the modern world in which we now live; at least as far as the possibilities of communications are concerned. On 21 December 1912, the *Daily Telegraph* carried a piece about Sir Hubert von Herkomer, a leading light of the fledgling British motion picture industry. He said:

> If one might indulge in a little chimerical phantasy, I should say that the day will come when the one film will take up form,

> colour and sound, and reproduce all these simultaneously; that
> a cinematograph will be laid on in every home, as your gas and
> electricity is now laid on . . .

All of which sounds uncannily like the cable television and Internet which makes cinema films available to us, just indeed in the same way that gas and electricity are laid on in our homes. This prediction was made at a time when most films were flickering, silent, black–and–white productions that one had to visit a cinema or music hall to see.

It is not too fanciful to suggest that visions such as this gave those working in the field of cinema a template or ultimate goal towards which they worked until the dream came to fruition in our own time; a century later. What about an international system for connecting everybody on the planet and ensuring that the world is drawn together by some kind of electronic communications network? There are even a set of initials for this visionary system; WWW. This is not a reference to the World Wide Web, but rather an earlier incarnation whose name might subliminally have inspired Sir Tim Berners-Lee to coin the expression in the first place, when he came up with the idea of the World Wide Web in 1989.

In 1902 Lee de Forest, at whose life and work we have already looked, teamed up with a shady businessman called Abraham White. The two of them launched a company called American De Forest Wireless Telegraph Company. One of the stated aims of this company was the development of what they called 'World-Wide Wireless'. Marconi had also used this expression; even abbreviating it to WWW! Of course, it was not merely chance phrases such as WWW from the early part of the twentieth century which have somehow drifted down to us over the years. These words and ideas often expressed themselves in the form of practical inventions which spurred technology on to create the world we know today. Consider this article, which appeared in the *New York Times* on 24 February 1907. It begins:

> Not long ago a popular writer on electricity made this startling
> prediction of coming wonders: 'Lovers conversing at a great
> distance will behold each other as in the flesh. Doctors will examine
> patients' tongues in another city, and the poor will enjoy visual trips
> wherever their fancy inclines. In hot weather, too, alpine glaciers
> and arctic snows will be made visible in sweltering cities, and when
> piercing northeast winds do blow, we shall gloat over tropical vistas
> of orchids and palms.'

After discussing the development of television, twenty years before John Logie Baird's first demonstrations, the article went on to speculate that one day

> it will surely be possible for the eminent surgeon in New York to see a bullet embedded in the body of a patient in Chicago or San Francisco; a combination of the X Ray apparatus and Dr Korn's invention will render this and even greater wonders mere commonplaces in our lives.

The idea that 'lovers conversing at a great distance will behold each other as in the flesh', reminds us today of such thoroughly modern practices as Skyping.

It is a little disconcerting that newspapers over a hundred years ago were containing speculations which are as accurate as those from the *New York Times* in 1907. The idea of Skyping, the notion that 'poor' people could enjoy images and films of faraway lands in the comfort of their own homes, even the amazingly modern and up-to-date concept of doctors diagnosing patients over the Internet and by sending X-rays along wires from one city to another. Rudimentary it may have been, but the device dreamed up by Dr Arthur Korn, the Professor of Physics at Munich University referred to in this newspaper article, paved the way for many of the features of the world which we take today for granted, from television to the Internet. What was this invention which was believed in 1907 to be about to revolutionize society?

Throughout the nineteenth century, there had been attempts to send pictures and text along wires, by means of electricity. It may come as a surprise to learn that some of these early experiments were so successful that the fax machine predates the telephone! In the late 1830s, a Scottish crofter's son called Alexander Bain began inventing a series of extraordinary electrical devices, some of them very much in advance of their time. One of these was a system for setting up a network of electric clocks, all of which would be kept in perfect time with each other. A master clock was placed at the railway station in Edinburgh and the pendulum of this clock set up so that every time it reached the end of the swing, it sent a signal along a telegraph line to a similar clock at the station in Glasgow. This powered a solenoid which ensured that the pendulum of the clock in Glasgow was perfectly synchronized with the one in Edinburgh. In this way, any number of clocks could all be kept running together and as long as the master clock was accurate, all the others would also be.

It was the fact that clocks separated by many miles could be guaranteed to operate in step like this, which gave Alexander Bain his next idea, which he called an 'electrochemical telegraph' and which we know today as the fax machine. Reasoning that if he had two pendulums at some distance from each other but both swinging in perfect unison, then it should be possible to use these for some means of communication. He came up with a scheme that involved turning pictures or print into an etched copper plate so that some parts stood proud from the surface. If an electrically-charged stylus or brush passed over such a plate, touching it very lightly, then the raised parts caused a current to be carried along a wire. If this stylus was attached to a swinging pendulum, then it would be possible to synchronize this to another pendulum miles away. This second pendulum, also carrying a stylus, would be passing over electro-sensitive paper, so that when a current flowed, the paper would turn black. When there was no current, the paper would remain white.

Bain's primitive machine was cumbersome and complicated, but it worked. As early as the 1840s, it was possible to transmit images along a telegraph wire. Within twenty years, a more sophisticated method had been devised in France and the world's first commercial fax service opened between Paris and Lyons in 1865. At about the same time, an experimental line was set up in Russia, between Moscow and St Petersburg. These systems, like that invented by Alexander Bain, relied upon a pendulum which swept a stylus across a prepared metal plate.

Obviously, having to convert every picture and piece of text into an engraving or otherwise producing a special version of an original was never going to be much use for a commercial undertaking. It would only be worthwhile if a copy of an original document could just be scanned straight away and transmitted as it was. Which is where Arthur Korn's Bildetelegraph came in. Korn's system was purely electrical, consisting of a glass cylinder containing a selenium cell.

Selenium is an element with a very curious property. In darkness, it will not conduct electricity at all. When light shines upon it, its conductivity increases in direct proportion to the amount of light present. By attaching to the glass cylinder the text or image to be sent and then focusing a beam of light upon it and turning the cylinder, Korn found that he was able to scan a copy by rotating the cylinder. The light passing through the image and the cylinder and then falling upon the selenium cell within was varied according to whether it was passing through a dark or light part of the picture fixed to the cylinder. This meant that a current passing through the selenium was constantly fluctuating and those variations in the strength of the current were sent through a telegraph line to a receiver which might be hundreds or even thousands of miles away. There, the electric current passed through a galvanometer and controlled the strength of an electric lamp. This is turn was shone into a camera and the varying intensity of the light reproduced, as the beam swept back and forth, the original image. The selenium cell was used of course in the first television, that constructed and demonstrated by John Logie Baird. During the years between 1901 and 1914, Arthur Korn's Bildetelegraph laid the foundations for Baird's work in this field. He foresaw the future and helped bring it into being.

Even with all its defects, Korn's system was of great use. The first picture transmitted over a wire in this way was a portrait of the German Crown Prince Wilhelm. On 17 October 1906, this was sent over a thousand miles and was printed clearly at the other end. Among early adopters of the system were the police. In August 1907, the cashier of a bank in the German city of Stuttgart absconded with something in the region of £2,000, equivalent today to about £75,000. He was thought to have taken a train for London, possibly travelling under a false name. The police in Stuttgart sent photographs of the wanted man to London via the receiving station there and Scotland Yard had them seven hours before the boat-train arrived at Charing Cross. There was no difficulty in identifying the cashier as he tried to slip through the barrier.

Illustrated newspapers such as the *Daily Mirror* were very keen on the new way of getting photographs to their office without delay. They began using a service set up between Paris and London and found that a photograph taken in Paris could be printed in London only two hours after the shutter had clicked. The quality of such reproductions was not always very good, but it meant that they could be first with the news, which was, after all, what being a newspaper is all about.

Television itself, or at least the word and preliminary models, was known years before John Logie Baird. It was a Russian, Konstantin Persky, who first used the expression 'television' at the World Exposition in Paris in August 1900. Before then, people had been speculating about the invention of a device which would allow live, moving images to be sent over through wires or via radio waves, but nobody had come up with a simple word. Both 'remote viewing' and 'electric telescopy' had been mooted, but neither phrase had caught on.

Arthur Korn and Alexander Bain both successfully sent still pictures along telegraph wires, but this was a slow business. There was great interest in the years immediately preceding the outbreak of the First World War in coming up with a method for sending live, instantaneous images electronically. This was first achieved in 1909. Both Korn's method of scanning by means of a selenium cell and Lee de Forest's triode amplifier made this possible.

Working in Paris, two researchers called Rignoux and Fournier arranged sixty-four selenium cells in an eight-by-eight configuration, rather like an extremely simply retina. Each cell was wired up individually to the transmitter. At the other end, a spinning disc with mirrors attached to the edge at various angles was struck by a beam of light modulated by the varying currents from the selenium cells. The light was then projected onto a screen. It was an exceedingly crude arrangement, but it proved possible to send individual letters of the alphabet through this system, the image from the eight-by-eight pixel receiver being refreshed several times a second. Two years later, very indistinct live images were sent through wires by a further refinement of this system.

Sending text and images from place to place through wires and on radio waves is obviously an important part of everyday life today and it has been interesting to look at the early origins of the practice. Another significant area of communication today is of course telephony; the electrical transmission of speech from one individual to another. Today, there are very few people in the United Kingdom who lack access to a telephone or other device such as a laptop, whereby they are able to speak to people across most of the world. This all but universal connectedness is a relatively recent development. It was only as late as 1975 that more than half the households in Britain had telephone lines. At that time, one of the first questions asked of a new acquaintance would be, 'Are you on the telephone?' The spread of the telephone and Internet in the last few decades has been due to the increasing use of fibre-optic cables, which are more efficient than copper wires at carrying information. Essentially, information is converted into pulses of light from lasers and then decoded at the other end of the line.

Sending telephone conversations along beams of light in this way sounds thoroughly up-to-date and modern, but it has its origins in research carried out in Britain during the 1870s, just a few years after Alexander Graham Bell patented the telephone in 1876. In October 1878, A.C. Ball first succeeded in sending speech along a beam of light in London. This was seen as being little more than a novelty, with no practical application. It was Bell who, realizing the potential of this idea, produced what he called the photophone. A small, flexible mirror mounted next to a tube served as the microphone for this revolutionary type of telephone. When words were spoken into the tube, the vibration caused the mirror to oscillate backwards and forwards. A beam of sunlight was directed onto the mirror and then reflected towards a receiver. At first, the receiver was simply a coating of lamp black, which varied slightly in conductivity as the modulated beam of sunlight fell upon it. Bell said that this was very effective; he described the speech received in this way as being, 'painfully loud'. But soon selenium, the same material used for sending photographs along electric wires, was found to be the most efficient way of turning the beam of light back into speech.

Bell's first work with the photophone took place in 1880 and the apparatus may be seen in Illustration 1. He thought, right up to the time of his death, that the photophone was the most important invention of his life, far eclipsing the electric telephone which is more usually associated with his name. After conducting his experiments in 1880, he wrote to his father, saying, 'I have heard articulate speech by sunlight! I have heard a ray of the sun laugh and cough and sing!' He was so excited at this invention that he wanted to call his baby daughter Photophone. His wife demurred and they named her Marian instead.

The problem with the photophone was that it was strictly limited in its range, and at a time when radio was coming into prominence, the idea of sending telephone calls a few hundred yards along a beam of reflected sunlight looked to be very much a blind alley. For a time, there were hopes that the photophone could replace all the hundreds of miles of straggling telephone wires with which city streets were increasingly festooned in the United States. The chief problem was that transmissions by light in this way could easily be disrupted by rain, fog, snow and other types of unfavourable weather. It was true that the quality of speech, under ideal atmospheric conditions, surpassed that obtained through copper wires, but then how often were those optimal conditions available? At least conversations on the telephone at that time were not likely to be interrupted because of a little rain!

In the years before the First World War, both the British and Germans recognized the military potential of the photophone, known also as the radiophone. Both nations, however, grasped that while it was dependent upon sunny weather, it was indeed little more than a toy. There were of course no lasers around in Edwardian Europe and so the most powerful source of light at that time, the carbon arc lamp, was used. In this way, the range of the photophone could be extended at night from a few hundred yards to seven or eight miles. This meant that commanders in the field or ships at sea could talk to each other without the hazards associated with radio or telephones. One can eavesdrop on both those methods of communication, but in the case of the photophone, any attempt to intercept the message would be immediately apparent, as the light beam would be cut off and it would be obvious that something was amiss.

There were intermittent attempts to revive the use of light-based communication throughout the twentieth century. Infra-red beams, of the kind which we use in remote controls to operate our television sets, were used by the Germans during the Second World War, but like the earliest photophones, the use of these was restricted by needing a clear line of sight and of course they could not operate over the horizon. It was not until lasers were developed after the Second World War, combined with the invention of fibre-optic cables in the 1970s, that the idea of telephone conversations being carried for great distances by a beam of light became a practical proposition.

The principle that information may be carried on pulses of light was, as we have seen, well known in the first years of the twentieth century. Something else that was well known was that there was a demand for news bulletins, weather forecasts and entertainment carried into people's homes via dedicated cables. Today, around 95 per cent of people living in the United Kingdom can access cable television. There was no television in the Edwardian period, but music and the spoken word were being carried directly to subscribers by wires installed for this purpose. In London, Rome, New York and Budapest what were known at the time as 'telephone newspapers' were growing in popularity. To describe these cable services as 'newspapers' is misleading. They were effectively radio programmes which, rather than being broadcast, were piped directly into the homes of those prepared to pay for the service. It was the Edwardian equivalent of cable television.

In London and Paris, talking newspapers were transmitted over ordinary telephone lines and a fee was charged for every connection to the service. In the Hungarian capital of Budapest though, special one-way wires were run into homes so that they could receive *Telefon Hirmondo*. This translates roughly as 'Telephone Herald', which was, incidentally, what a similar service in New York was later named. Because the amplification of electrical signals was in its infancy at that time, those wishing to listen to these 'talking newspapers' had to wear headphones. An article from an American magazine, published in 1901 when the Hungarian service was flourishing, describes how 5,000 kilometres of wire carried the *Telefon Hirmondo* service to 6,200 homes in Budapest. These days, the cables carrying broadcasts to subscribers are usually buried beneath the pavement, but at that time they were hung on poles and ran into the eaves of houses. A look at the programme schedule reveals that this talking newspaper was almost indistinguishable from a modern radio station. The morning timetable began as follows:

9.00 Precise time signal
9.30 Foreign news
10.00 Stock Exchange quotations
10.30 Roundup of local news headlines
11.00 General news and finance

Microphones were positioned permanently in the Budapest Opera House, which meant that subscribers to *Telefon Hirmondo* could enjoy listening to the opera in the evening, relayed live into their homes.

In London, a service similar to *Telefon Hirmondo* operated between 1895 and 1925. This was provided through the ordinary telephone lines; at first working in conjunction with the National Telephone Company and then the Post Office, when they assumed responsibility for providing telephone lines. The British system was called Electrophone and at its height had around 2,000 subscribers. Most of the programmes were transmitted live from London theatres and the service could also be listened to in hotels on a pay-as-you-go basis. Queen Victoria was an Electrophone customer.

The 'Talking Newspapers' in Europe and America relied upon either a telephone line or a specially-installed cable. This made them the exclusive province of the well-to-do, an upper or middle-class pastime. In America, a soldier called George Owen Squier devised a new system, one which was to have huge implications for communications technology and has proved crucial in the modern world for providing us with telephone, television and the Internet through cables. It is called multiplexing and without it, our world would be a very different place indeed.

The 'Talking Newspapers' at which we just looked all needed a separate line for each person, just as was the case with telephones at that time. It had been known for some time though that it was possible to send more than one message along a wire. This was routinely done with telegraph lines and by the end of the nineteenth century things such as duplex, the simultaneous carrying of messages in both directions along a telegraph wire, were well known. Applying the same idea to the spoken word or music was a different thing entirely though and it was George Squier who solved the problem when he patented what he described as 'wired wireless' - a contradiction in terms, if ever there was one!

Major George Owen Squier was an officer in the United States Army Signal Corps before the First World War. He was a forward-looking man who was very interested in new inventions which might have some use for the army. In 1908, he became one of the first aeroplane passengers in history, when he allowed Orville Wright to take him aloft in the flimsy Wright Flyer. At once, Squier recognized the military potential of aircraft. He could look down on the ground and see what was happening below him and also see far further into the distance than was possible at ground level. There were of course observation balloons but these new mobile, fast-moving vehicles were infinitely more useful from a military perspective.

Returning to his interest in telecommunications, Squier found that using copper wires, for example telephone wires, as guides, enable radio to be carried a long distance with no loss of quality or interference from static. The wires were being used as wave guides. Sending radio along telephone wires like this did not affect any conversations being carried by the wires themselves. This discovery was made as part of Squier's work with another important feature of modern telecommunications, that of multiplexing. It had already been known for some years that more than one telegraph message could be sent simultaneously along a line. In 1910, Squier found that the same thing could also be done with telephone wires and that one wire could carry many calls at the same time. This discovery led to his being elected to the National Academy of Science.

The idea of 'wired wireless' was very similar to the telephone 'broadcasts' at which we looked above. It was intended that radio transmissions would be carried not through the air, in the way with which we are today familiar, but along the ordinary wires which carried electricity into people's homes. This was done by means of decoder boxes which were bought from the company, precisely in the way that we now have little boxes which allow us to receive cable and satellite television.

The advantages of Squier's 'wired wireless' in the early days of radio would have been considerable. Early transmissions were masked by crackling static and receivers, other than simple crystal sets, tended to be very cumbersome, with batteries consisting of accumulator jars which had to be regularly recharged. Programmes sent along a wire suffered no degradation and were as clear as when they left the studio. The problem was that by the time that 'wired wireless' really took off, radio receiving sets had grown more reliable and sophisticated. If you could receive broadcasts from all over the world for free, why pay for one of Squier's boxes, which would give you access only to one station?

Nothing daunted, as soon as Squier realized that radio stations through wires was not going to be the success that he hoped, he switched direction and decided instead to provide what we now know as 'piped music' to commercial clients, rather than trying to persuade people to pay to have it delivered to their homes. Impressed by how snappy the trade name 'Kodak' was for cameras, he decided to come up with something as catchy for his own project. By taking the first syllable of the word 'music' and then combining it with the last syllable of 'Kodak', he came up with the word 'Muzak', a name to send a chill through the hearts of older readers!

Muzak became a feature of life in America, where it was piped into factories and other workplaces to boost productivity. Slow, quiet music would gradually increase in volume and pace until workers found themselves unconsciously speeding up their output. In Britain, it was chiefly encountered in shops and hotels, where it provided what was known as 'mood music'. This widely disliked manifestation of post-war life in industrialized nations had its origins in Edwardian technology.

It is in the nature of analogue copies and communications to fade and corrupt. This is the case with photographs on film, radio broadcasts, gramophone records, tape recordings and everything else. The reason is that analogue copies are only imprecise facsimiles to begin with and any slight variation will serve only to make them even less accurate imitations of the original than when they were first produced. Radio waves can be distorted and blocked, records become scratched, photographic negatives can be smudged or obscured by water or dirt.

The case is altogether different with the digital world. The strings of binary digits are a bit like Morse code, virtually indestructible signals. They can be switched into different forms and sent along wires, through the air as radio waves, as pulses of light through fibre-optic cables, stored on magnetic hard drives or in the network of microscopic transistors which we call flash drives or memory cards. Once you have that string of digits, you are able accurately to reconstruct perfectly the original music, text, photograph or film. Photographs might become torn and stained, but the collection of binary digits which make up an image from a mobile telephone or digital camera can be stored in a hundred places and will always appear as a perfect image.

Very old analogue recordings of music or speech are almost invariably degraded and faint. We might hear Florence Nightingale or Alfred Lord Tennyson speaking, but must strain our ears to pick out the words above the crackling and hissing of the phonograph cylinder's imperfect recording.

Similarly, there exist gramophone and phonograph recordings from the late nineteenth century which feature well-known musicians playing their compositions. They have a certain novelty value, but it is almost impossible to listen to those ancient recordings without wincing. The quality of reproduction is truly execrable.

Of course, all this changed with the introduction of compact discs in the 1980s. Music on these was recorded by microscopic pits burned, and also read, by lasers. This digital information, a series of dots and dashes, was accurate and permanent. The age of digital music had arrived and analogue music recordings began their slow decline in popularity. As conductor Herbert von Karajan said of this new medium in 1983, 'All else is gaslight!' Strangely enough though, the early 1980s did not really mark the dawn of digital music recordings at all; they had actually been around for almost a century by that time. The Norwegian composer Edvard Grieg died in 1907, but digital recordings exist of him playing his piano concerto and they are as crisp and clear today as when they were made over a hundred years ago. There is no distortion, no crackling and the sound is as loud as though he were really playing in the same room. Listening to these digital recordings 110 years after Grieg's death is an uncanny experience.

To understand how the digital recording of music began, it is necessary to look back to the end of the eighteenth century, when musical snuffboxes were being produced by skilled watchmakers in Europe. These evolved into the familiar music box. A little spiked cylinder or disc revolved and raised protrusions or pins plucked at a tuned steel comb. The result was pleasing to the ear, if a little tinny. The traditional music box is of course an example of digital technology. Only ones and zeros are present; there is no midway point or graduation. Some of these music boxes were quite complex, not only using miniature plectra to sound a melody, but also featuring little drums too. These are some of the earliest examples of digital music.

As the nineteenth century advanced, music boxes were produced in ever larger sizes, until some examples were the size of gramophones. These came with interchangeable cylinders or discs, so that an endless variety of music could be enjoyed by a well-to-do family. This was the home entertainment centre of the day. Families gathered round the music box to listen. Sounding boards were fitted to the things, so that the music was loud enough to dance by or sing an accompaniment to them. Among the most famous manufacturers was the German company Polyphon, who made cabinet-sized music boxes for which extra discs could be purchased. They were the digital record players of the late nineteenth and early twentieth century. Polyphons, which were driven by clockwork, were installed in public houses in Britain during the years prior to the First World War. When a penny was put in them, they would play popular melodies; they were an early kind of jukebox. Here is a description of such an early jukebox from the novel *The Ragged-Trousered Philanthropists,* written in 1909. Describing the interior of a public house, the author says that, 'A large automatic musical instrument – a "penny in the slot" polyphone – resembling a grandfather's clock in shape – stood against one of the partitions and close up to the counter, so that those behind the bar could reach to wind it up.'

All of which brings us to the recording of digital music. Some readers might have felt that all this talk about the old-time music box being a digital device is a bit of an exaggeration or play on words, but the music box gave rise to things such as the programming of computers by means of punched tapes, a method used well within living memory. Music boxes, even the grand versions produced by companies such as Polyphon, always have a distinctive, metallic sound to them. During the nineteenth century, the piano was the most popular musical instrument to be found in people's homes. Listening to it being played was an evening pastime for many, both in Britain and the rest of Europe. How if it became possible to get a piano to play automatically in the same way that a music box does?

The chief problem about operating a piano like a music box is that there is more to piano-playing than simply striking the keys. The force with which the keys are struck affects the performance, as does the length of time that the key is held down. With a music box, the pin or other metal protrusion simply plucks the steel comb with the same force each time, giving a mechanically repetitive feel to the music produced in this way. It is clear that a machine is at work. Hearing a piano played in this way would bring no pleasure to anybody! Alexander Bain, whose efforts at devising the first practical fax machine we looked at earlier in this chapter, wrote about using a moving sheet of perforated paper as a 'travelling valve' to operate the reeds of an organ, but this was no use for a piano, which requires considerable force to bring the hammer down on the strings inside the instrument.

As electrical power began to be used more widely, automatic pianos were developed in which the holes in a paper roll were read and a circuit completed, which allowed an electromagnet to raise and let fall the hammers linked to the keyboard. Further work in this field resulted in the player-piano, which would play by itself when a roll of music was fed in. These proved tremendously popular around the turn of the century and there were even 'format wars', similar to the way in which the VHS/Betamax video systems fought for dominance in the 1980s. In this case, the disputes ranged around whether the rolls should allow for the playing of all eighty-eight notes or merely sixty-five. The width of the paper and the number of holes per inch also varied from one manufacturer to another. In the end, everybody agreed a standard format for the rolls, but not before some of the smaller firms which had invested heavily in the wrong format were driven out of business.

The breakthrough in player-pianos came with the launch of the Welte-Mignon reproducing piano in 1904. For the first time, this allowed accurate recordings to be made of an individual performance. Not only the notes were recorded on the paper roll, but also the timing, phrasing and use of pedals, along with faithfully copying the exact pressure used on each key and the length of time which it was depressed. In short, the entire dynamic of a piece of music played on the reproducing piano could be copied and made into as many punched-paper tapes as one might require. Famous musicians and composers were eager to be commissioned to have their playing immortalized for all time.

There is a case for seeing the widespread use of the Welte-Mignon piano as the first digital music revolution. There's no doubt that the list of musicians who queued up to have their playing recorded in this way is an impressive one. Grieg, Paderewski, Mahler, Debussy and Rachmaninoff were among the composers whose recordings we still have. Popular musicians like George Gershwin, 'Jelly-roll' Morton and Scott Joplin also made rolls for the public to buy. Old gramophone recordings from that time have often degraded to an alarming degree, but run one of those punched tapes through the appropriate device today and one can hear Paderewski playing exactly as he did a century ago; with no distortion or interference.

The perforated tapes used in player-pianos became the programming system of choice for computers in the years following the end of the Second World War. Although superseded today by hard drives and memory sticks, the perforated paper tape which contained information had its origins in the player pianos of the Victorian and Edwardian eras.

As a matter of fact, there was an earlier use of paper tape to programme machinery and it too contributed to the Analogue Revolution in Edwardian Britain. In Chapter 3 we learned about the Linotype machine, which made the printing of newspapers so much quicker and cheaper than ever before. Shortly after the Linotype was launched, Tolbert Lanston set up a business in the United States called the Monotype Machine Company. This was to exploit a new composition system which Lanston had patented in 1885. The Monotype was a little slower than the Linotype, but was programmed by a paper tape, whose holes contained the information on letters and spacing. A keyboard operator typed out the text and as he or she did so, the information was automatically punched onto a paper tape. Spacing could be more finely controlled on the Monotype and mistakes more easily rectified. It was the Monotype which really caused the art of designing typefaces to take off, and hand-cutting of moulds for this system triggered the start of modern typography.

Another example of the way that something which we regard as being quintessentially up-to-date and modern, although it has really been around for a century or so, lies in the use of radio to communicate with aeroplanes. The British Army was carrying radio sets into battle and using them to coordinate their troop movements during the Boer War. Five bulky radio sets were mounted in horse-drawn vans and were being used in South Africa as early as 1899, but the loose, dry soil was hopeless for establishing the necessary 'earth' connection and the experiment was not really a success. In 1903, the Royal Navy used radios with kite-borne aerials in the campaign in Somaliland. Britain was also very quick off the mark in using radio to communicate with aeroplanes. Flashing signal lamps and flags had previously been the only way of sending messages between the ground and a plane in flight. On 27 September 1910, a Bristol Boxkite biplane took part in army manoeuvres on Salisbury Plain. It carried a radio transmitter weighing 14lb. This could of course only send Morse, but while in mid-air, the pilot managed to transmit messages to a station on the ground.

There is a common, strange and wholly inexplicable belief that 'instant' cameras, those capable of producing photographs which can be viewed less than a minute after they are taken, appeared for the first time after the Second World War and were developed by Edwin Land and his Polaroid Corporation. We are most of us familiar with the story of how Land took a photograph of his little daughter and the child's disappointment on learning that she would not be able to see the picture at once, but would have to wait days for it to be developed in a darkroom. This story, touching and heart-warming as it may be, is very misleading. The 'instant' photograph arrived many decades before Edwin Land took the snapshot of his daughter and the type of camera able to produce such pictures reached the peak of its development a year or two before the outbreak of war in 1914.

Illustration 19 shows a German camera which went on sale in 1912. This futuristic-looking contraption was invented by Romain Talbot, a German photographer, and used ferrotype plates to produce developed photographs in a minute or so. Ferrotypes, sometimes known as tintype photographs, were thin iron sheets which were painted or enamelled black and coated with a thin photosensitive layer. Because of the black background, ferrotypes provided a direct positive print. Like the later Polaroids, only one copy was produced, rather than a negative from which any number of prints could be made. Because there was only one step in the process and also because the metal plates did not need to be hung up to dry, as was the case with paper prints, ferrotype pictures could be developed very swiftly. In the late Victorian period, photographers set up booths at seaside resorts and took pictures of holidaymakers which could be ready in a matter of minutes. All that was needed was to dip the exposed plate into a tank of developer and then rinse it off.

The magazine camera, which was pioneered independently in Germany and America, streamlined the whole ferrotype process until there was no need for a booth, with its darkroom and tanks of chemicals. Typically, these cameras had a magazine which held dozens of little metal blanks, each no larger than a button. When the portrait had been taken, the blank dropped automatically into a bath of developer held in the base of the camera. The finished photograph was ready to hand over to the customer in a minute. The pictures taken with these miniature portrait cameras were either fixed to a badge or inserted into a large, cardboard frame for display. Because they were so small, they were known either as buttons or gems.

Some instant cameras being marketed at this time took larger pictures. The Mandel brothers, Louis and Manuel, were running the Chicago Ferrotype Company and selling what they described as 'one minute picture-taking machines', as early as 1907. Their cameras produced both the small button or gem type prints and also the more conventional two-and-a-half by three-and-a-half-inch plates.

We see that forty years before Edwin Land's daughter was so taken aback to find that she would have to wait to see her photograph, cameras were being widely used across Europe and America which allowed people to see their pictures almost as soon as they had been taken. Land was essentially tinkering with a device which had been on sale at least two years before he was born in 1909!

Another type of photographic apparatus which was around a lot earlier than is generally supposed was the photocopier. Making copies of letters and drawings had always been a time-consuming business and one inevitably prone to error. At the beginning of the nineteenth century, everything was copied laboriously by hand, but with the invention of typewriters and carbon paper, it became easier to produce copies of a document as the original was made. Carbon copies, though, tended to smudge and become indistinct if handled too often and as the twentieth century dawned, there was still no easy way of copying an existing plan, drawing or document.

True, there were a number of copying machines on the market, such as the mimeograph and, from 1891 onwards, the cyclostyle, but these relied upon waxed stencils and messy chemicals. Making copies of drawings and plans was a particularly time-consuming process. A quick look at the commonest way of reproducing drawings and plans, the blueprint, will served to illustrate how difficult things were before the introduction of photocopiers.

The word 'blueprint' is today used to mean simply a plan or original outline of some idea or scheme. Many people don't know that blueprints were actual, physical objects, nor that making them was a complex, messy and unsatisfactory process. If one had an architect's drawing that one wished to copy, then there were two basic ways that this might be done. The first of these was to engage a skilled draughtsman to make a precise copy of the thing, something which might easily take half a day or more, but from the 1860s onwards, another method could be used. If a large sheet of specially-prepared paper is coated in a solution of ferro-gallate, it becomes sensitive to light. The coating as applied is yellow, but exposure to sunlight will cause this lemon-yellow to darken to a rich blue.

A copy in Indian ink was first made of the drawing or plan which had to be copied. This was made on translucent tracing paper. A sheet of sensitised paper was then clamped under a sheet of glass and the tracing secured above it. This would then be placed outdoors for a few minutes, whereupon it would be seen that the paper coated with ferro-gallate was darkening to a cobalt blue. The copy would then be taken indoors and washed, to remove any remaining ferro-gallate which had not reacted to the light. The result would be a blueprint; a sheet of blue paper with the original black lines showing in white.

Apart from the need for mixing up solutions of chemicals and coating paper with them, then later washing off the remaining solution after exposure to light, there was also the need for a careful tracing to be done by hand before the blueprint could be made. One further difficulty with the blueprint process was that soaking the paper twice and coating it with chemicals had the effect of making it very brittle. Blueprints could not be folded or even handled roughly, or else they were liable to crack. It was necessary to keep them in special portfolio folders and to handle them as gently as possible.

What was needed was an easier method of copying plans, maps, drawings and documents without first having to prepare special copies. A quick, easy and clean way was needed of turning out as many copies as were required of an original. Two companies, both based in the United States, solved this problem simultaneously in 1907.

Few people today remember the Rectigraph Company, founded in Oklahoma City by George Beidler. The other company to go into business that year producing commercial copiers has become a household name, its trade name becoming a generic term. Just as many people refer to all photocopies as 'xeroxes', so too did the expression 'photostat' pass into the language to denote any document issuing forth from an office copier; by whomever the machine might have been manufactured. The Photostat machine was the first office copier and it could make quick and accurate copies of any pictures or text.

The Photostat machine, which incorporated a copying camera, was invented by the American Oscar T. Gregory in 1907. A few years later, he set up the Commercial Camera Company to exploit his invention. By 1912, one had been installed in the New York Public Library and another part of the modern world as we know it had emerged. It may seem surprising to learn that photocopiers were appearing in libraries before the First World War, but the basic design of the machines relied upon principles which had already been known for many years.

The Photostat machine consisted of a large camera, which could produce images either at life-size or various reductions or enlargements. There was no need for any complex calculations by the operator to reproduce a document at, say for example, 75 per cent. The person making the copy simply moved the bed where the document lay to a certain position on a scale marked with the required reduction or enlargement.

The beauty of the Photostat was that one only needed to wait for a few seconds to collect the finished copy. We looked earlier at the development of 'instant' cameras, long before the 'Polaroid' was marketed. Photostat machines used similar methods, on a slightly larger scale. They were loaded with 350-foot long rolls of sensitised paper and when the copy had been made, the paper passed through tanks of developer and fixer, before being dried by an electric fan. The first copy to emerge was a negative and this could then be copied as many times as necessary. The whole process, from laying the document in the machine to collecting the copy, took just thirty seconds. Illustration 20 shows an advertisement for a Photostat machine from 1913. It mentions that one company turned out 160 copies in just an hour and twenty minutes. The photocopier revolutionized work in offices and meant that many draughtsmen and technical artists were made redundant in the years following its introduction and widespread use.

We will end this chapter by looking at two military uses for radio which both had their roots, surprisingly, before the First World War. The first of these are two of the most up-to-date weapons which feature regularly in the news today; cruise missiles and so-called 'drones'. In our own time, we have seen how new inventions are often combined in novel ways. The digital camera and the mobile telephone, for instance, or light-emitting diodes and digital television signals. In 1910, aeroplanes and radio were both exciting new developments in communications and travel, and it was perhaps inevitable that somebody should have come up with the idea of linking them together.

At New York's Madison Square Garden in 1898, inventor Nikola Tesla demonstrated something which to most of those watching seemed little short of magic. In a large pool of water, Tesla placed a model boat, one which was fitted with miniature lamps on its mast. He then proceeded to manoeuvre the little vessel around the pool, even flashing its lights on and off at will. Most of the audience had not even heard of radio and even had they done so, they would certainly have been unable to conceive of a way that it might be exploited like this, to steer a boat. Yet that was all that Tesla was doing from his mysterious black box; sending out invisible rays which operated the rudder and lights of the boat.

When aeroplanes began to appear, first in the United States and then later in Europe, the idea was soon mooted of controlling them too by radio. This is much more difficult though than steering a boat, where essentially a rudder must only be moved one way or the other. Aeroplanes move in three dimensions and if anything goes wrong, the consequences are likely to be severe. If a boat malfunctions, it will generally remain afloat. An aeroplane though is likely to plunge from the sky, to the hazard of those on the ground. Before a pilotless aircraft could be built, a method would need to be found to keep it flying in a stable way, even when it was out of sight of the person controlling it. The solution to this challenge was an ingenious one and has today become an integral part of our lives. Every smartphone in the world uses the invention which made remote controlled and automatic flight possible.

From 1896 onwards, experiments were being undertaken, principally in America and Germany, to find a reliable way of finding the direction of travel at sea. Magnetic compasses point not to true north, but to the Earth's magnetic north. The further north a vessel travels, the more that the difference between true and magnetic north matters. The other problem with magnetic compasses on board a large boat is that they are affected by the ferrous metal of the hull. The solution to both these problems was to develop a gyroscopic compass, one which would point in the required direction at all times and anywhere on Earth.

We are most of us familiar with the gyroscope as a novelty or toy. Once set spinning rapidly, its angular momentum will cause it either to continue pointing vertically upright, or at any angle at which it is placed. The movement of the surface upon which it stands will not affect the orientation. This means that if a gyroscope can be pointed at true north and set spinning, then it will keep pointing in that direction, no matter what.

The breakthrough in producing a practical gyrocompass was made simultaneously in 1907 by two men, one working in America and the other in Germany. German scientist Hermann Anschutz-Kaempfe needed to perfect the gyrocompass for a planned expedition of a submarine which would pass under the Arctic ice. For any voyage so close to the Earth's magnetic north, an ordinary compass would be useless. By 1908, just as American Elmer Sperry was also perfecting and patenting his own gyrocompass, Anschutz-Kaempfe was selling his own version to the Imperial German Navy. Both men claimed to have invented the gyrocompass and there were a lot of patent disputes in the following years.

Elmer Sperry set up the Sperry Gyroscope Company in 1910 to market his own gyroscopic stabilisers and gyrocompasses. These, like those of Hermann Anschutz-Kaempfe, were maritime aids to navigation; Sperry's earliest gyrocompasses were fitted aboard US Navy destroyers. However, Sperry began to turn his attention to the problem of navigation and control of aeroplanes; in particular the possibility that an aircraft could be controlled from the ground by radio. This was ground-breaking work indeed, dealing as it did with three very new technologies; those of radio, aeroplanes and gyrocompasses. As with the naval use of gyrocompasses, both in America and Germany, it was the armed forces who were likely to be the customers for such a development.

Going off at a slight tangent, although still on the subject of information and communication technology, gyrocompasses are now used every day by most people in the developed world. Anybody using a smartphone will have noticed that the image on the screen mysteriously orients itself, according to whether the phone is held upright, in the so-called 'portrait' position, or lengthways.

When mobile phones are used to play certain games, driving simulators for instance, the phone knows when it is being slanted to one side or held vertically. All this is accomplished by means of tiny gyroscopes, which sense the movement of the phone and are able to measure changes of position with great accuracy. Those early electrically-driven gyroscopes from Edwardian America and Germany, originally devised for such things as submarine voyages in the Arctic, have evolved into essential components of our everyday lives.

That any large radio-controlled aeroplane would need gyroscopic stabilisers or gyrocompasses was neatly demonstrated on 21 March 1917, when British officer Captain Archibald Montgomery Low of the Royal Flying Corps attempted to show a group of generals how his invention for destroying Zeppelins worked. It was the height of the First World War and the giant German airships had been bombing Britain for some while. Captain Low had devised a pilotless aircraft which could be used as a flying bomb. The first public flight of Low's unmanned plane took place on Salisbury Plain. Low had not thought it necessary to use gyroscopic stabilisers for his aeroplane, which was launched by compressed air from the back of a lorry. However, a slight variation in movement caused the airborne weapon to veer off course, turn sharply and then dive straight towards the startled generals; who were forced to run for their lives. Nobody was injured, but Low's ingenious device was completely wrecked. The slightest instability in the path of an aeroplane which had no pilot to make the necessary adjustments proved disastrous. The need for some kind of stabilisation was never more apparent.

In America, Elmer Sperry had more success in building remotely-controlled bombs, as his aeroplanes were all fitted with gyroscopes from the beginning. Things like drones and cruise missiles seem so modern, that it comes as a bit of a surprise to find that they were being developed in the years before the First World War. The cruise missile in particular is a state-of-the-art piece of military hardware whose sole aim is to fly many miles to a target and then blow it up. Who would imagine that the Edwardians were working on such a project? By 1918, the remotely-controlled plane had evolved into a flying bomb, indistinguishable from today's cruise missiles. Both radio-controlled and automatic versions had emerged from the experimental work and the flying bombs had a theoretical range of over fifty miles. For a while, it was hoped that some of these could be used to attack German submarine bases, but they were never sufficiently accurate and reliable. By the end of the First World War, winged bombs with warheads weighing 1,000lbs had been tested. The only problem was that although they could be sent many miles, the navigational equipment was not quite accurate enough for military purposes. They proved unable to be able to strike specific targets. Detonating 1,000lbs of high explosives within half a mile of a warship or fortress, which was the greatest accuracy achievable, was not really much use. After the war ended, the weapons programme continued for a few years, before grinding to a halt as government interest in funding military projects gradually decreased.

One final instance of radio technology in use before the First World War might be of interest. Although not primarily devised with military applications in mind, this particular invention proved to be of the utmost importance during the Second World War, enabling Britain to survive the onslaught of the *Luftwaffe* in 1940 and thus deter the Nazis from invading. Radar is traditionally thought of as being a secret weapon of the British during the opening months of the war and many of us have the impression that it had been developed in secret as a way of protecting the country from unexpected air raids from German bombers flying in from across the Channel. The truth is that radar was a German invention and one which had been patented in 1903, almost forty years before the Battle of Britain.

On 21 November 1903, a 22-year-old German inventor filed a patent application in Berlin. Christian Hulsmeyer had previously worked on a method for setting off explosive charges by radio, sending sounds over a telegraph line and several other strange projects. He was convinced, though, that his latest idea was to be a real winner. The description of the invention contained in the patent application was as follows:

> Hertzian-wave projecting and receiving apparatus adapted to indicate or give warning of the presence of a metallic body, such as ships or trains, in the line of projecting such waves.

Hertzian waves was at that time a common way of describing radio waves. Hulsmeyer's invention was essentially radar. The only thing which he failed to mention in the patent was that this new machine could also be used to spot approaching aeroplanes. Since the first powered flight of a heavier-than-air flying machine would not take place until three weeks after he had made his patent application, we may perhaps forgive Christian Hulsmeyer for this omission!

The telemobiloscope, for so Hulsmeyer named his invention, consisted of a spark-gap transmitter to generate radio waves and antennae to send them in a particular direction. Reflected signals were captured in a parabolic antenna, a little like a modern satellite dish of the kind that are commonly seen today fixed to houses. When incoming signals were detected, they triggered the ringing of an electric bell. The apparatus could be pointed precisely and aligned with a compass. The range of the target could be calculated by using two detectors at different heights and then carrying out trigonometric calculations to find the distance of the object which was reflecting the radio waves.

The telemobiloscope was, like the gyroscopic compass, intended to make navigation at sea easier and safer, the idea being that a ship could be aware of other vessels nearby at night time or during a fog. Once he had found a financial backer, Hulsmeyer arranged for practical demonstrations of his ingenious system. After the first public display of the telemobiloscope in May 1904, when it was shown to be able to detect the iron gate of a hotel in Cologne, it was time to test its efficiency on real ships. This was duly done at Rotterdam on 9 June 1904. Those present, including representatives of large shipping companies, were satisfied that the telemobiloscope was perfectly capable of signalling when a ship passed within range of its detector.

Despite this initial success, the company which Hulsmeyer had set up to exploit his invention went into liquidation in 1905. There were several reasons for this. Many ships now carried wireless sets, which interfered with the operation of the telemobiloscope, sending it false and misleading signals. There was also the indisputable fact that foghorns and lights were more effective than this primitive radar scanner, whose range was limited to a mere two or three miles. It would be another thirty years before interest was revived in the idea of detecting distant vehicles by means of radio waves and then it would be aeroplanes rather than ships which would be the focus of engineers working on the idea.

In this chapter, we have seen that the Edwardian period saw the birth of many of the gadgets and devices which we today take for granted, ranging from televisions and radar to cruise missiles, piped music and the gyroscopes which orient the screens of our smartphones correctly. There are few aspects of modern information and communication technology which were not either being experimented with or at least dreamed of in those heady years between the death of Queen Victoria and the outbreak of war in the summer of 1914. All the modern manifestations of these inventions are of course digital, rather than analogue, but the ideas themselves are rooted firmly in the Edwardian era.

Chapter 10

The Enduring Legacy of the Analogue Revolution

We are today accustomed to what seems to us to be an indisputable fact: that the hardware which is the external manifestation of our information revolution is all of a fleeting and ephemeral nature. The computers and mobile telephones of even fifteen or twenty years ago, to give but one example, look absurdly outdated. In 2009, the Blackberry was the epitome of cutting-edge communications; within five years, with its fiddly little keys, it looked like a museum piece. The same is true of the bulky cathode-tube computer monitors and television sets which were ubiquitous a couple of decades ago. All have now been consigned to the dustbin of history and replaced with flat LED and plasma screens.

Some of the machinery of the information and communications technology upon which we now rely has risen rapidly for a few years and then sunk without a trace. In the late 1980s, many people acquired telephone answering machines, which recorded messages on miniature cassettes. They seemed so up-to-date and modern; flashy gadgets which had previously only been seen in offices. Today, only a few years later, they are as outdated as carbon paper. Many readers will remember how futuristic floppy discs seemed in the 1990s - keeping our records on them was certainly the way that modern people did things. Today, you will literally not see any device using floppy discs outside a museum!

The rapidity with which communication and information technology becomes outdated may be seen elsewhere; in cars, furniture and clothes, for instance. Many things in the modern world have built-in obsolescence; within two or three years, five at the most, they will need to be replaced with something a little more up-to-date. This 'planned obsolescence', as it has been called since the 1950s, is today a fact of life. Through advertising and little tweaks in design and appearance, things we bought only three or four years ago can be made to feel hopelessly old-fashioned. Most of us get rid of mobiles or cameras long before they have worn out or broken down. Manufacturers know this and so use cheaper components which will not last longer than five years or so. This keeps down prices and so makes the article more competitive in the marketplace. After all, why make something to last if it will be thrown in the dustbin anyway after a few years?

In addition to this, of course, we are still in the midst of an information revolution and have not yet reached the plateau, where the technology we are using will remain stable for a long period. The changes that we see happening constantly around us have the effect of making things seem incredibly old, even after ten years. It is barely thirty years since the first newspaper pictures were printed in colour. When they appeared in 1986, they were a sensation. At that time, British newspapers were still working with the Linotype machines which had been in service for almost a century. Today, black-and-white newspaper pictures look as quaint to the modern eye as sepia-tinted daguerreotypes!

Thinking of the fact that in the mid-1980s British newspapers were all using Linotype machines brings us neatly to the point of this chapter, which is that in addition to the length of time that the basic designs of the analogue revolution persisted, there was also the astonishing durability of the physical manifestations of the information technology perfected during the Edwardian period. Until just thirty years ago, almost all the machinery used for printing, typing, communicating across distances and for the recording of images and sound had scarcely changed since the beginning of the First World War and not only that, but in many cases the actual devices used at that time were still extant. An example will illustrate this point.

Illustration 8 shows the keyboard of a newspaper Linotype machine. There is something odd about this keyboard and it takes us a little while to noticed what it is. It is so obvious that it might not strike one immediately, but the letters are not arranged in the standard way with which we are today familiar. This is not a QWERTY keyboard. The arrangement here is ESCVX. The QWERTY layout was devised in the 1870s, by a newspaper editor called Christopher Sholes. It took a few years to become the standard way of laying-out the keys of a typewriter. The keyboard in Illustration 8 is of a Mergenthaler Linotype machine made in 1888; it was constructed in the days before QWERTY had become the universally-accepted way of arranging keys. The truly astonishing thing about this machine is that it was still in use at the *Washington Post* until 1980! In short, this simple and robust piece of analogue technology was beavering away in a newspaper office from the late Victorian Age until the modern era of computers. This is durability. It is difficult to believe that any of the machinery currently installed at the *Washington Post* will still be in use in 2110!

The Edwardian information revolution, which has been referred to in this book as the Analogue Revolution, was very swift. It covered a period of less than twenty years and at the end of that time, the basic information and communications technology that had been developed would remain unchanged until the start of the digital revolution of our own lifetimes. The recording of images on photographic film by cameras with mechanical shutters, the gramophones, the tape recorders, the Linotype machines, the electro-mechanical telephones, radios and typewriters; all followed precisely similar principles to their counterparts in 1910. The outward form of the cameras and telephones might alter over the years, but the underlying technology did not. This may be seen by the fact that some products of the Edwardian information revolution, such as the Linotype machine mentioned above, were still in use as late as the 1980s.

In an earlier chapter, we looked in detail at Kodak's famous Box Brownie camera. This iconic camera was so cheap and was produced in such quantities, that many were still floating around eighty years after it was launched in Britain at a cost of 5/- (25p). This meant that battered old models of the Box Brownie were still turning up in junk shops and at jumble sales throughout much of the twentieth century. They were not generally regarded as items that any serious collector might want, unless in especially fine condition, with the original paper sleeve showing the Brownie, for example. In the early 1980s, on the very cusp of the digital revolution, one could acquire an original Box Brownie, in working order, for less than £1. Even more surprisingly, the film for these cameras could still be bought at any chemists.

The Box Brownie is no isolated example of the robustness of Edwardian information and communications technology and its ability to endure for almost a century. Just as it was possible to pick up a Box Brownie for a nominal sum in the 1970s or 1980s, so too with typewriters from the early part of the twentieth century. Imposing Underwood machines were also to be found in junk shops, often lingering in the windows for months or years, because nobody had any interest in them. The ribbons for such typewriters, just like the films for Edwardian cameras, were freely available and with a new ribbon, those machines would, perhaps with a little tinkering, be able to function as well as they had done before the outbreak of the 1914–18 war.

Mention of 'tinkering' with a typewriter brings us neatly to one of the reasons that the tools of communication used by the Edwardians were still going strong until the age of computers. They were all based upon simple and easily understood principles and could be adjusted and repaired by ordinary people if they malfunctioned. This was an important consideration when buying something like a typewriter; which in real terms would have been terrifically expensive in 1910. Nobody would wish to buy a costly machine and then when it went wrong, find that repairing it was an expensive or impractical undertaking. Manual typewriters of the kind that were popular in Edwardian Britain were essentially made up of simple and easily-understood pieces of machinery – levers and springs in the main. If a lever jammed, then it could usually be twisted by hand to realign it to the correct position. Sticking parts could be oiled, springs replaced and so on.

It is amusing to compare the idea of fixing a manual typewriter with the notion in our own time of finding out what is wrong with an inkjet or laser printer and setting it right! The technology which we use today to produce a page of text is immeasurably more complex than that used by the Edwardians. This is reflected of course in the price. In 1982, just as the current information revolution was taking off, a manual typewriter bought from a high-street shop like W.H. Smiths' cost about £35. This would enable the average person to turn out many hundreds of pages of text: the ribbon on such a typewriter could be used over and over again, until the words became too blurry and faint to read. These days, a single ink cartridge for a printer can easily cost about the same amount. Of course, buying a typewriter was a one-off, whereas the purchase of ink cartridges is a regular expense. If a printer goes wrong, a not uncommon occurrence, then most people simply throw it out and replace it with a newer model and so, in a sense, that too is a recurring expense which must be factored in when we are working out how much it costs us to use this technology.

The fact is that people in the developed world, of which Britain is part, now have far more money to spend than has ever before been the case. For this reason, there is no incentive for any manufacturer to produced things which can be mended, whether we are talking of cameras, watches, shoes or hairdryers. If they go wrong, we throw them away and buy a new one. This attitude is a very recent development and one which would have been incomprehensible to most people for almost the whole of the twentieth century. This accounts in part for the durability and standardisation of so many of the technological developments in the early years of the century; people just wouldn't have bought things like cameras and typewriters if they weren't going to last.

There is another reason why information and communications technology seemed to stand still for much of the twentieth century; it is a manifestation of the inherent conservatism of most people. When something works well enough, whether it is Parliamentary democracy or the cameras which we take on holiday, we tend to stick with the old and avoid the new; at least until we see if other people are going to change too! By the mid-1980s, the London thoroughfare of Fleet Street had been associated with printing for nearly 500 years, ever since William Caxton's apprentice Wynkyn de Worde set up a printing press at premises at the junction of Fleet Street and Shoe Lane. There had, in the nineteenth century, been opposition to the installation of both steam-driven rotary presses and the then Linotype machines, but this settled down and for a century, the British national newspaper industry remained virtually unchanged, both in terms of geographical location and the technology being used. There was no good reason for staying in that small and limited district, any more than there was to avoid trying out new advances in the field of printing. Nevertheless, nobody felt inclined to change; it was easier to carry as they had been doing for the better part of a century, staying in the same place and using the old, familiar machinery.

When, in 1986, a new national newspaper was published by means of computers, doing away with the need for printers and their Linotype machines, there was uproar. We pause at this point and look once more at Illustration 8, which shows the keyboard of an old Linotype machine of the sort still being used in the 1980s. This keyboard was used continuously for nearly a century. In 1986, the year that the new *Today* newspaper began using computers and featuring colour photographs, Rupert Murdoch moved production of the *Times* and *Sun* to Wapping, also starting to use new methods to print these newspapers. It was by these means that the newspaper industry was dragged, quite literally screaming and protesting, into the modern age. A similar, if gentler, process took place in other fields. Often, the difficulty lay not in the technical advances but rather in the reluctance of people to accept change. As observed above, most people preferred to carry on using manual typewriters, cameras with film and telephones with dials.

Of course, the amazing robustness of the products of Edwardian industry was by no means limited to information technology; it was built into every aspect of the machinery made during that time. An example will illustrate this point neatly. Between 1967 and 1977, Britain gradually stopped using gas produced from heating coal and began using natural gas from the North Sea. As a result, all gas cookers, fires and so on had to be adapted for use with the new gas. It was an enormous undertaking, which entailed visiting almost every business and home in the country. In the course of the enterprise, it was discovered that not only cookers and fires needed to be altered so that they could be used for natural gas. Quite a few people still relied upon gas lighting in their homes!

It is hard to believe, but even as late as the 1970s, Edwardian light fittings were still in regular use in people's homes. Some of them had been in daily use for seventy or eighty years, without the occupants of the houses having seen any need to upgrade to electric lighting. It had all been working smoothly since the end of the nineteenth century and there had been no technical problems in that time. It is unlikely that any homes today will reach the twenty-second century without changing their lighting system or experiencing any difficulties. In those days, they built things to last; whether those things were telephones and cameras or domestic lighting systems.

One noticeable difference which has taken place in respect of our relationship to the technology of everyday life is that most people no longer have the faintest idea how their cameras, printers and telephones work. In 1980, the man or woman with a manual typewriter could see at a glance how it operated and what might be going wrong with it – if it would no longer type the letter 'A', for example. The key with the little image or representation of the letter 'A' on it was at the end of a little lever, which was in turn connected to a longer lever. This second lever had at the end of it a metal copy, in reverse, of the letter 'A'. Banging the picture of 'A' on the key with your finger caused the first lever to swing the longer lever and make it spring forward and swing hard against a strip of material impregnated with slightly damp ink. This allowed the metal print-face to mark an 'A' on the paper. There could hardly be a simpler way of printing letters on a piece of paper.

If something went wrong with a manual typewriter, it was often something which might be remedied without too much fuss. Perhaps a drop of oil might be needed, so that the metal parts slid more smoothly against each other or maybe a spring needed to be replaced. It was usually immediately apparent what the nature of the malfunction was when watching the thing in operation. Compare this situation with working an inkjet or laser printer. Few of us even know how the letters are caused to appear on the paper when using such a machine, let alone what might go wrong or how we might fix it! The earlier machines were also very resilient and resistant to damage. Manual typewriters were made of metal and could be dropped, have cups of tea spilt on them and generally be mistreated in a hundred other ways without being irreparably damaged. Try that sort of thing with a modern printer and you will soon see the difference.

When an exceedingly rugged and familiar technology has served you, your father and grandfather well, there is little incentive to change it. Why invest in an electronic typewriter when a manual one is much cheaper, sturdier and likely to outlast the fancier model which can only be used when electric power is available? Newspaper reporters carried portable manual typewriters all over the world and did not need to worry about fading batteries or power cuts.

Today's information and communication technology is, as we have seen, predicated upon the tacit assumption of built-in obsolescence. Nobody buying a laptop today seriously expects to be able to bequeath it to his son. We know that within five years, ten at the most, the thing will either have stopped working or that new programmes will mean that our computer is on its last legs. Telephones have an even shorter span and so, by implication, do cameras. Most people use their mobiles now to take pictures, rather than go to all the fuss and bother of carrying around a separate electronic gadget. How long do we keep our phone for? It was once a point of pride to boast of how long a camera or typewriter had lasted. Today, the opposite is true; the pride consists of telling people how new these things are.

This frame of mind, in that even as we acquire some new electronic device that that we accept that it will be discarded in a few years, five at the most, is a strange one and would have been quite unfamiliar until perhaps twenty or thirty years ago. Anybody buying a decent camera in the 1980s would expect it to last, if not forever, then probably for the lifetime of the person making the purchase. A Hasselblad or Pentax camera was built of metal and glass and with care could easily last for fifty years. Much the same would have been felt about the acquisition of a typewriter. It was simple and robust and there was no reason to suppose that it would ever stop working. All that would be necessary was to change the ribbon from time to time.

We have talked of information and technological revolutions as being periods of great and rapid development, culminating in plateaux where things remain much the same for many years until the next phase of change occurs. The same cycle may be seen in other areas, transport, for instance. During the nineteenth century, steam locomotives were introduced and then changed very greatly between Stephenson's *Rocket*, built in 1829, and those being constructed fifty years later. Compare a steam engine from 1890 with one from 1960, though, and you will find that they are all-but indistinguishable. This is because the phase of rapid development ended and throughout the twentieth century, until the replacement of steam locomotives by diesel and electric trains, the plateau had been reached and nothing much was done with the designs of such things. The same thing applied, by and large, to telephones, cameras, typewriters and gramophones.

From the reign of Edward VII to the 1990s, there was little or no change in the construction of cameras. They used similar, in some cases identical, films, the methods used to increase and decrease the aperture remained unchanged, the mechanism which moved the film forward each frame, even the basic arrangement for opening the back of the camera to insert the film was the same in 1999 as it had been in 1909. There was no need to change any of this; it worked perfectly. This is an example of a technological plateau. The mechanism worked well and there was no scope for improvement. Typewriters too worked on the same principle in the 1890s and in the 1980s. Perhaps they were built of lighter material in the latter part of the twentieth century, the case might have been of plastic instead of metal, but the basic design was identical. This was another technological plateau.

Even when the concept of 'planned obsolescence' came to the fore in the 1950s, there was no rush to apply it to information and communication technology. What would have been the point? Nobody would invest in a new typewriter unless the latest model offered some radical new advantage over the one already possessed. And so the typewriters, cameras and radios which had been in families for years still lingered on in homes. Sometimes, they would be handed on to the next generation. A couple setting up home might perhaps be given a radio which had been giving good service for years or, after the death of a parent, children might feel it worth having a camera or typewriter which had been in use for forty years or more.

Endword

Examining the past can sometimes tell us a good deal about the present and even give us hints about the probable course of the future. This may be the case when studying the Edwardian Analogue Revolution and its aftermath. An awful lot happened in the way of information and communication technology between 1900 and 1914. The foundations were laid for the methods we would use to communicate over distances and store information for the next eighty or ninety years.

If an Edwardian scientist could have been transported in a time machine from 1910 and brought to the year 1990, most of what he was shown in the field of long-distance communications and information storage would have been perfectly comprehensible to him. He would see cameras using film coated with silver iodide, typewriters which worked by banging little metal letters against an inked ribbon, telephones which were, apart from their external appearance, identical to those which he himself was in the habit of using. Radios and record players would all operate on familiar principles. Even the things with which he was unfamiliar, such as fax machines and televisions, would not be all that mysterious. He would most likely have come across the idea of them, mooted perhaps in scientific magazines of his day and it would not take him long to grasp the mode of operation. Other things, such as incandescent electric light bulbs, would not have changed at all in the eighty years which had passed since his own time.

Consider the situation now if instead of delivering our time traveller to 1990, we had brought him forward another few years to the present day. Now, he is likely to be utterly perplexed by the everyday devices which he sees in use. Digital cameras will relate to nothing at all that he knows and nor will an inkjet printer. Even the light bulbs will be puzzling. LED lights, plasma screens, digital radio, laptop computers, smartphones; none of this will have the least connection with the science of his own world. It will seem almost like magic!

We began the first chapter of our exploration of this topic with a quotation, that from L.P. Hartley's *The Go-Between*, 'The past is a foreign country; they do things differently there'. Perhaps we should end with another quotation, this time from George Santayana: 'Those who cannot remember the past are doomed to repeat it.' We are in the habit of viewing our own time as being in some sense the culmination of scientific endeavour and achievement. We are persuaded that we understand the true nature of the universe and are on the verge of creating life itself. The fabulous discoveries that science has made are amply shown in our day-to-day lives. Just look at the incredible inventions which fill our homes today and that we even carry round in our pockets!

This feeling, that one's own age has reached a peak of knowledge and science which can never be bettered, is common to the periods of rapid invention and development which we call information revolutions. We start to believe that there is nothing much else to invent and that all we can hope for are refinements and improvements in the technology which we are already using; an even thinner mobile telephone, for instance, or a television which might be unrolled like a poster and hung on any convenient wall as easily as we hang a picture. That the very nature of our technology will change radically at some point and leave us unable to grasp what has happened seems to us, at this stage, a foolish notion. This was precisely how many people felt during the Edwardian information revolution. Consider this quotation from the magazine *Scientific American* on 2 January 1909:

> That the automobile has practically reached the limit of its development is suggested by the fact that during the past year no improvements of a radical nature have been introduced.

The strange belief that scientific progress has now reached its limits is often found at the beginning of an information revolution. It goes hand in hand with the exhilarating mood which causes people to think that civilization has now reached some ultimate pinnacle. Here are one or two more examples of this peculiar delusion. Two years before the world of physics was rocked to the core by the publication of Albert Einstein's theories on relativity and the quantum nature of light; an eminent physicist had decided that everything useful was already known about physics. Albert Michelson said in *Light Waves and their Uses*, published in 1903:

> The more important fundamental laws and facts of physical science have all been discovered, and these are so firmly established that the possibility of their ever being supplanted in consequence of new discoveries is exceedingly remote.

It is not only scientific discoveries and inventions which people are often persuaded have reached their highest points during information revolutions; such times typically bring forth predictions as well that political and social conditions are almost perfect as well and that the world will no longer be changing much in any way at all! Consider American political theorist Francis Fukuyama who, shortly after the fall of the Berlin Wall in 1989, and just as the digital revolution of our own times was beginning to pick up pace, wrote a singularly foolish essay called *The End of History*. In it, he expounded the view that capitalism and democracy were now triumphant and so there would be no further conflict and history had essentially come to a natural conclusion. He wrote:

> What we may be witnessing is not just the end of the Cold War, or the passing of a particular period of post-war history, but the end of history as such; that is, the end-point of mankind's ideological evolution and the universalisation of Western liberal democracy as the final form of human government.

A rash claim indeed and just the sort of thing which people often get into their heads when they see a new information revolution taking hold. A mad optimism grips the world and it is easy to believe that all these wonderful new scientific discoveries and inventions mean that Utopia is just around the corner.

The idea that the world will now be a better place for everybody and that the usual round of wars and upheaval has now come to a permanent halt was also in the air during the Edwardian information revolution. We may compare Fukuyama's extravagant words with those of Guglielmo Marconi in October 1912, when he was quoted in *Technical World Magazine* as saying that 'The coming of the wireless era will make war impossible, because it will make war ridiculous.' Less than two years later, the First World War began, which saw slaughter on a scale unparalleled in human history.

It has been worth examining the story of the Analogue Revolution, if for no other reason than for the light which it can shed on our own age. Our study of past information revolutions, especially that which took place between 1901 and 1914, has shown that such upheavals are invariably followed by periods where nothing much happens in the field of information and communication technology for decades, or even centuries, until the next such revolution. Rather than the constant upgrades of our computers and exciting hew gadgets which seemingly pop up every other day, we shall soon be reaching a plateau: a time of consolidation and stagnation where nothing much will happen for decades. Such an idea is as inconceivable to us as it would have been to the Edwardians. Certainly, there were new inventions in the decades following the Analogue Revolution, things such as television, but these were essentially developments of existing technology and television sets used the same valves and amplifiers as were to be found in radio sets.

We cannot imagine the end of the digital revolution, nor can we have the faintest idea what will succeed it. What is quite certain though is that just as the technology of the Edwardians slowly became antiquated and unable to cope with the demands of the modern world, so too will our modern devices eventually become obsolete and a little absurd. The day will surely dawn when the smartphone and iPad will looks as quaint and antiquated as candlestick telephones and Bakelite wireless sets.

Bibliography

Anstey, A.E., *Vice Versa*, Elder Smith, 1882.

Auer, Michael, *The Illustrated History of the Camera*, Fountain Press, 1975.

Beyer, Rick, *The Greatest Stories Never Told*, A&E Television Networks, 2003.

Briggs, Asa, *A Social History of England*, The Viking Press, 1983.

Cannon, John (ed.), *The Oxford Companion to British History*, Oxford University Press, 1997.

Challoner, Jack, *1001 Inventions that Changed the World*, Cassell Illustrated, 2009.

Cohen, Morton, *Lewis Carroll*, Alfred A. Knopf, 1995.

Cook, Chris, and Stevenson, John, *Modern British History 1714-1980*, Pearson Education, 1983.

Dodgshon, Robert A., and Butlin, Robin A., *An Historical Geography of England and Wales*, Academic Press Inc, 1991.

Gilbert, Martin, *A History of the Twentieth Century*, Harper Collins, 2007.

Gregory, Yvalanna, *Marjie – The True Story of an Edwardian Girl*, ShieldCrest, 2013.

Grimley, Gordon, *The Origins of Everything*, Mayflower Books, 1973.

Harmer, Harry, *The Labour Party 1900-1998*, Addison Wesley Longman, 1999.

Harris, Melvin, *Book of Firsts*, Michael O'Mara Books, 1994.

Hart-Davis, Adam, *Eurekaaargh!*, Michael O'Mara Books, 1999.

Hattersley, Roy, *The Edwardians*, Little, Brown, 2004.

Homer, Trevor, *The Book of Origins*, Piatkus Books, 2006.

Jerome, Jerome K., *Three Men on the Bummel*, J.W. Arrowsmith, 1900.

Le Queux, William, *The Invasion of 1910*, E. Nash, 1906.

Marr, Andrew, *The Making of Modern Britain*, Macmillan, 2009.

Marriot, Emma, *Bad History; How We Got the Past Wrong*, Michael O'Mara Books, 2011.

Moorehead, Alan, *The Russian Revolution*, Time Inc., 1958.

Moynahan, Brian, *The British Century*, Weidenfeld & Nicolson, 1997.

Opie, Robert, *The Edwardian Scrapbook*, Pi Global Publishing, 2002.

Palmer, Alan, *The Penguin Dictionary of Twentieth Century History*, Penguin Books, 1979.

Platt, Richard, *Cinema*, Dorling Kindersley, 1992.

Powell, David, *The Edwardian Crisis, Britain, 1901–1914*, Macmillan, 1996.

Priestley, J.B., *The Edwardians*, William Heinemann, 1970.

Rayner, Ed, and Stapley, Ron, *Debunking History*, Sutton Publishing, 2002.

Roberts, Pamela, *The Genius of Colour Photography*, Carlton Publishing, 2007.

Robertson, Patrick, *The Shell Book of Firsts*, Ebury Press, 1974.

Robinson, Andrew, *The Story of Writing*, Thames & Hudson, 1995.

Slee, Christopher, *The Guinness Book of Lasts*, Guinness Publishing, 1994.

Standage, Tom, *The Victorian Internet*, Weidenfeld & Nicolson, 1998.

Sweet, Matthew, *Inventing the Victorians*, Faber and Faber, 2001.

Tressel, Robert, *The Ragged-Trousered Philanthropists*, Grant Richards, 1914.

Webb, Simon, *Dynamite, Treason and Plot: Terrorism in Victorian and Edwardian London*, The History Press, 2012.

Index